S - A N O N

Twelve Traditions

S-ANON
International

Family Groups

S-Anon Twelve Traditions
© S-Anon International Family Groups, Inc., 2022

Library of Congress Catalog Card Number: 2021917884
ISBN 978-0-9676637-9-1
SAN: 255-0261

S-ANON
International

Family Groups

S-Anon Conference Approved Literature
Printed in the United States of America.

For information contact the S-Anon World Service Office:
S-Anon International Family Groups, Inc.
P.O. Box 17294
Nashville, TN 37217-0294
Phone: 615-833-3152 Toll-Free: 800-210-8141
Email: sanon@sanon.org
Website: www.sanon.org

God, grant me the serenity

To accept the things I cannot change,

Courage to change the things I can,

And wisdom to know the difference.

ACKNOWLEDGMENTS

❧

The excerpts from *Alcoholics Anonymous*, the Big Book are reprinted with permission of Alcoholics Anonymous World Services, Inc. (A.A.W.S.) Permission to reprint these excerpts does not mean that A.A.W.S. has reviewed or approved the contents of thispublication, or that A.A. necessarily agrees with the views expressed herein. A.A. is a program of recovery from alcoholism only — use of these excerpts in connection with programs and activities which are patterned after A.A., but which address other problems, or in any other non-A.A. context, does not imply otherwise.

Grateful acknowledgment is made for permission to reprint the following:

Excerpt from *Alcoholics Anonymous*. Copyright 1939, 1955, 1976, 2001 by Alcoholics Anonymous World Services, Inc.: New York, NY. Reprinted by permission of Alcoholics Anonymous World Services, Inc.

Excerpts from *Reflections of Hope*. Copyright 2008, Second Reprinting 2020 by S-Anon International Family Groups, Inc.: Nashville, TN. Reprinted by permission of S-Anon International Family Groups.

Excerpts from *Working the S-Anon Program*. Copyright 2003, 2009, Second Edition, Second Reprinting 2021 by S-Anon International Family Groups, Inc.: Nashville, TN. Reprinted by permission of S-Anon International Family Groups, Inc.

CONTENTS

❧

S-ANON PREAMBLE
TO THE
TWELVE STEPS

 ❧

S-Anon is a fellowship of people who share their experience, strength, and hope with each other so that they may solve their common problems and help others to recover. The only requirement for membership is that there be a problem of sexaholism in a relative or friend. There are no dues or fees for S-Anon membership; we are self-supporting through our own contributions. S-Anon is not allied with any sect, denomination, politics, organization or institution; does not wish to engage in any controversy; neither endorses nor opposes any causes. Our primary purpose is to recover from the effects upon us of another person's sexaholism and to help families and friends of sexaholics.

S-ANON TWELVE STEPS

❧

1. We admitted we were powerless over sexaholism—that our lives had become unmanageable.

2. Came to believe that a Power greater than ourselves could restore us to sanity.

3. Made a decision to turn our will and our lives over to the care of God *as we understood Him.*

4. Made a searching and fearless moral inventory of ourselves.

5. Admitted to God, to ourselves, and to another human being the exact nature of our wrongs.

6. Were entirely ready to have God remove all these defects of character.

7. Humbly asked Him to remove our shortcomings.

8. Made a list of all persons we had harmed, and became willing to make amends to them all.

9. Made direct amends to such people wherever possible, except when to do so would injure them or others.

10. Continued to take personal inventory and when we were wrong promptly admitted it.

11. Sought through prayer and meditation to improve our conscious contact with God *as we understood Him,* praying only for knowledge of His will for us and the power to carry that out.

12. Having had a spiritual awakening as the result of these Steps, we tried to carry this message to others, and to practice these principles in all our affairs.

THE TWELVE STEPS OF ALCOHOLICS ANONYMOUS

1. We admitted we were powerless over alcohol — that our lives had become unmanageable. 2. Came to believe that a Power greater than ourselves could restore us to sanity. 3. Made a decision to turn our will and our lives over to the care of God *as we understood Him*. 4. Made a searching and fearless moral inventory of ourselves. 5. Admitted to God, to ourselves, and to another human being the exact nature of our wrongs. 6. Were entirely ready to have God remove all these defects of character. 7. Humbly asked Him to remove our shortcomings. 8. Made a list of all persons we had harmed, and became willing to make amends to them all. 9. Made direct amends to such people wherever possible, except when to do so would injure them or others. 10. Continued to take personal inventory and when we were wrong promptly admitted it. 11. Sought through prayer and meditation to improve our conscious contact with God *as we understood Him*, praying only for knowledge of His will for us and the power to carry that out. 12. Having had a spiritual awakening as the result of these Steps, we tried to carry this message to alcoholics, and to practice these principles in all our affairs.

S-ANON TWELVE TRADITIONS

✎

1. Our common welfare should come first; personal progress for the greatest number depends upon unity.

2. For our group purpose there is but one authority — a loving God as He may express Himself in our group conscience. Our leaders are but trusted servants — they do not govern.

3. The relatives of sexaholics, when gathered together for mutual aid, may call themselves an S-Anon Family Group, provided that, as a group, they have no other affiliation. The only requirement for membership is that there be a problem of sexaholism in a relative or friend.

4. Each group should be autonomous, except in matters affecting another group or S-Anon or SA as a whole.

5. Each S-Anon Family Group has but one purpose: to help families of sexaholics. We do this by practicing the Twelve Steps of S-Anon, by encouraging and understanding our sexaholic relatives, and by welcoming and giving comfort to the families of sexaholics.

6. Our S-Anon Family Groups ought never endorse, finance, or lend our name to any outside enterprise, lest problems of money, property, and prestige divert us from our primary spiritual aim. Although a separate entity, we should always cooperate with Sexaholics Anonymous.

7. Every group ought to be fully self-supporting, declining outside contributions.

8. S-Anon Twelfth Step work should remain forever non-professional, but our service centers may employ special workers.

9. Our groups, as such, ought never be organized; but we may create service boards or committees directly responsible to those they serve.

10. The S-Anon Family Groups have no opinion on outside issues; hence our name ought never be drawn into public controversy.

11. Our public relations policy is based on attraction rather than promotion; we need always maintain personal anonymity at the level of press, radio, TV, and films. We need guard with special care the anonymity of all S-Anon and SA members.

12. Anonymity is the spiritual foundation of all our Traditions, ever reminding us to place principles above personalities.

S-ANON TWELVE CONCEPTS
OF SERVICE

༖

S-Anon's Twelve Concepts of Service illustrate that Twelfth Step work can be accomplished on a broad scale. The Concepts are guidelines for the World Service Office staff, the Board of Trustees, standing committees, and World Service Conference members to relate to each other and to groups.

1. The ultimate responsibility and authority for S-Anon world services belongs to the S-Anon groups.

2. The S-Anon Family Groups have delegated complete administrative and operational authority to their Conference and its service arms.

3. The Right of Decision makes effective leadership possible.

4. Participation is the key to harmony.

5. The Rights of Appeal and Petition protect minorities and assure that they be heard.

6. The Conference acknowledges the primary administrative responsibility of the trustees.

7. The trustees have legal rights while the rights of the Conference are traditional.

8. The Board of Trustees delegates full authority for routine management of the S-Anon Headquarters to its executive committees.

9. Good personal leadership at all service levels is a necessity. In the field of world service the Board of Trustees assumes the primary leadership.

10. Service responsibility is balanced by carefully defined service authority and double-headed management is avoided.

11. The World Service Office is composed of an executive director and staff members.

12. The spiritual foundation for S-Anon's world services is contained in the General Warranties of the Conference, Article 12 of the Charter.

The General Warranties of the Conference

In all its proceedings the World Service Conference of S-Anon shall observe the spirit of the Traditions:

1. That only sufficient operating funds, including an ample reserve, be its prudent financial principle;

2. That no Conference member shall be placed in unqualified authority over other members;

3. That all decisions be reached by discussion, vote, and whenever possible, by unanimity;

4. That no Conference action ever be personally punitive or an incitement to public controversy;

5. That though the Conference serves S-Anon, it shall never perform any act of government; and like the fellowship of S-Anon which it serves, it shall always remain democratic in thought and action.

(The Twelve Concepts of Service reprinted and adapted with permission of Al-Anon World Services, Inc. Permission to reprint and adapt the Concepts does not imply that Al-Anon is affiliated with this program. Al-Anon is a program of recovery from the effects of alcoholism. Use of this material in connection with programs which are patterned after Al-Anon, but which address other problems, does not imply otherwise.) S-Anon's Twelve Concepts of Service were formally adopted and approved at the first annual S-Anon World Service Conference January, 2004.

INTRODUCTION

❦

The S-Anon Twelve Traditions are spiritual guidelines that foster harmony and unity within our groups and throughout our worldwide fellowship. They provide a firm foundation for our program and our relationships and help us to interact in safe and healthy ways in all areas of our lives. The S-Anon Twelve Steps encourage us to learn to focus on ourselves; the S-Anon Twelve Traditions expand our vision to our relationships with others. Learning to relate to others in a respectful and appropriate way is a tremendous gift that comes to us from our Higher Power through the Traditions.

We have immense gratitude for those who have come before us. The Traditions were first developed through trial and error by Alcoholics Anonymous (AA) in response to situations that arose in their fellowship. AA wisely presented the Traditions as suggested guidelines, relying upon the spiritual aspect of the program to ensure that their fellowship would prevail. Early members of Al-Anon adapted the Traditions of AA to fit the needs of their fellowship. S-Anon members recognized their value and created the S-Anon Twelve Traditions by adapting those of Al-Anon. SAnon's Tradition Five differs by stating that we practice the Twelve Steps of S-Anon, whereas Al-Anon's Tradition Five refers to practicing the Twelve Steps of AA. Later, wording was inserted into Tradition Eleven to protect the anonymity of all S-Anon members as well as Sexaholics Anonymous members.

As in AA and Al-Anon, in S-Anon the Twelve Traditions are not considered rules. No one has authority to enforce them; instead, we speak of "obedience to the unenforceable." As stated in the S-Anon meeting format, "Our group experience suggests that the unity of the S-Anon Family Groups depends upon our adherence to the… [Twelve] Traditions."[1] With the help of our Higher Power, they suggest effective ways to make decisions, prevent many problems, and deal with issues that may arise. As we apply these principles to the way we conduct ourselves, we gain a deeper appreciation of the value of respect and humility within our S-Anon fellowship and in all our relationships.

S-Anon Twelve Traditions offers an in-depth study of important spiritual principles. Topics such as unity, common welfare, group conscience, requirement for membership, authority, group purpose, relationship to outside groups or institutions, responsibility, service, public relations, and anonymity are discussed in detail. The material for each Tradition is written from the S-Anon point of view and has been gathered from contributions of countless S-Anon members. The guidance of our Higher Power and the joint effort of members over many years have brought this book to fruition.

Each of the Traditions has its own chapter, which is divided into four sections. The first section is a description of the Tradition and presents basic information about how we can apply it to our lives both inside and outside the S-Anon program. The "Stories" offer personal experiences S-Anon members have had in using the Tradition in their groups as well as in their families and communities. Some of us might read these first two sections, yet find we still have some reservations, inner resistance, or uncertainty about how to apply the Tradition. The next section, "Practicing These Principles," addresses some challenges that we might have in embracing the principles of the Tradition. It helps us work through these impediments and continue to move forward in our recovery. The chapter concludes with the "Questions," which offer a framework for studying the Tradition and can be used for meeting topics, a

----

[1] *Working the S-Anon Program,* p. 115.

personal inventory, and discussions with a group, sponsor, or other program member.

Studying the S-Anon Twelve Traditions offers us an opportunity to embark upon a deeper and broader recovery journey. We invite you to experience, with the help of your Higher Power, the many benefits of learning about and practicing the Traditions in your S-Anon group, your personal recovery, and every other aspect of your life. Many gifts await you.

TRADITION ONE

✿

Our common welfare should come first;
personal progress for the greatest number
depends upon unity.

Our Twelve Traditions offer gentle suggestions about working together and providing a safe place for personal growth on our journey toward improving our relationships with others, including the sexaholic. When we consider our common welfare, we remember that S-Anon's primary purpose is to help families and friends of sexaholics. We think about our own needs, but we also take into account the needs and well-being of the entire group. When we relate to each other with respect, courtesy, and appreciation of our common welfare, we create a caring, spiritual community.

Learning how to relate to others while preserving our own autonomy is a tremendous gift that we receive when we work the S-Anon program. We all work together to make sure that our fellowship is healthy so it can continue to offer help, hope, and peace to those who have been affected by someone else's sexual behavior. Our personal progress depends upon a healthy fellowship. Therefore, we concern ourselves with our common welfare—what is best for the group as a whole—both for our own sake and the sake of other members.

Our S-Anon group may have been the first place where we experienced the principle of common welfare. We began to feel a sense of safety, unity, and stability, which is key to our successful interaction with other members and to our personal recovery. This might have seemed foreign to us, as most of us did not learn from our family of origin how to interact with others in a healthy way.

Often we came to S-Anon with a fractured sense of unity; living with sexaholism, whether or not we realized it at the time, left many of us feeling hurt, isolated, ashamed, afraid, and desperate. Our relationships with the sexaholics in our lives may have been very frustrating and confusing because of the lack of honesty and transparency. Our thinking became distorted. We learned to discount our value, to shut down, to fight to be heard, to keep peace at any price, or to employ other self-defeating behaviors. The pain of living with sexaholism may have caused such anger and resentment that we thought we did not need to treat the sexaholic with common courtesy, kindness, and respect. The idea of working in harmony with others may not have seemed familiar, comfortable, or even necessary; but in S-Anon, we can begin to feel a sense of peace, belonging, and connection with others who understand our difficulties.

In our S-Anon groups, as in all areas of our lives, sometimes we encounter people whom we find difficult; but if we keep an open mind, experience has shown that we can learn from everyone. Sometimes a person with whom we have least identified shares something that proves beneficial to our recovery.

One of S-Anon's spiritual principles is that we are all equal, and that our ideas are equally important. Sharing from newcomers is just as valuable as that of long-time members. Whether we share from the pain of recent discovery or from years of applying the principles of the program to our lives, our perspectives can benefit others. Our Higher Power can speak to us through anyone. If we open our minds and hearts, we can learn from each other.

Negative self-judgment and pride, two of the common effects upon us from living with or having lived with a sexaholic, can prevent us from sharing or from listening during our meetings. Regardless of our time in S-Anon, we find that if we invite our Higher Power to guide our words, we say what we need to say, when we need to say it. By doing so, we may positively impact other members. We gradually begin to trust that our group is a comfortable place to find our voice and practice our equality. This makes it easier for us to connect meaningfully with others. When we apply Tradition One, we create a harmonious atmosphere that makes us want to "Keep coming back."

Tradition One gently reminds us of our individual responsibility to observe the meeting guidelines and Traditions; by doing so, we preserve the unity and protect the health and survival of our group. We strive to remember our common welfare when sharing at meetings and listening to others. The guidelines wisely protect our common welfare and encourage us to keep the needs of the whole group in mind as we share our experience, strength, and hope. We remember that other members need time to share their pain or progress as well, so we are careful to limit the length of our sharing. We refrain from talking about the sexaholic's choices because that distracts us from our own recovery. We focus on our common experiences in recovering from the effects of sexaholism, rather than on our differences. Even though our circumstances might be different, our feelings and the effects of the disease on us are similar.

Our meeting guidelines help to create a safe environment where we can share who we were, who we have become, and what has helped us on our journey. We can share freely only if we feel safe, without fear of criticism, comments, advice, or gossip. When we allow others to share without being interrupted or judged, we provide a secure environment that fosters trust and regard for others. Each time we share or listen to another member share, we move farther from the darkness of isolation and despair and closer to the light of unity with other S-Anon members, where we find understanding, encouragement, and acceptance.

We do our best to be mindful of our primary purpose--to help families and friends of sexaholics. We avoid topics that may divide us and distract us from our common goal of S-Anon recovery. Therefore, during our meetings, we do not mention outside issues, including other Twelve Step recovery groups, therapies, politics, or religions. We also refrain from talking about specific titles, authors, or publications other than Conference Approved Literature (CAL). S-Anon literature aims to provide a clear and consistent guide to the principles of S-Anon recovery. Written by S-Anon members and passed through a rigorous approval process, S-Anon literature becomes a unifying element at meetings and encourages us to focus on the solution rather than on the problem. It offers us a new language to use to relate to each other. As we increase our understanding and sense of belonging, we forge a bond with our members worldwide who have traveled this road before us. Our exclusive use of CAL and a similar meeting format help us feel comfortable and welcome whether we are attending our regular "home" group or an S-Anon meeting anywhere else in the world.

S-Anon unity extends beyond our local, telephone, or electronic meetings, and includes our Intergroups, Area Delegates, Board of Trustees, World Service Office, and S-Anon members in other parts of the world. We benefit from the wealth of experience, strength, and hope we have found in this worldwide fellowship. Tradition One also guides us in our S-Anon service work. When members come together to plan an area or regional program or an International Convention, we focus our efforts on our common welfare and unity. All who have a problem of sexaholism in a relative or friend are invited and welcome to attend any S-Anon event. S-Anon is a *we* program as we work together to solve our common problems. Our message of recovery offers hope to those who have not yet come to meetings as well to S-Anon members everywhere.

Our understanding of S-Anon unity deepens when we study Tradition One and begin to apply its principles, not only to our interactions with other S-Anon members, but also to our interactions with those in our families, workplaces, and other areas of our daily lives. Keeping our common welfare in mind when we address issues, set goals, or make even the smallest decisions helps expand our focus. We learn to treat others as equals and give their opinions the same consideration we would like our opinions to receive. We can listen respectfully without interrupting. We admit that our way is not the only way, and we work together to find a solution that might better serve the good of all involved. We recognize that our personal desires are not always in the best interest of our groups, so we become willing to let go of our own agenda if it does not promote our common welfare. We begin to appreciate a sense of connection with and compassion for others with struggles of all kinds. We realize that our Higher Power cares for us all, no matter what our situation may be, and will always guide us as we apply these spiritual principles to all areas of our lives.

Tradition One provides a practical framework and a spiritual pathway for us to build respectful, productive, unifying, and safe relationships where our healing and growth can flourish.

• • •

Tradition One
STORIES

One of the first meetings I attended consisted of many members who seemed to have known each other for a long time. I observed that after each speaker shared, subsequent comments from other members included personal references to the speaker's sharing and the changes they had observed in the speaker throughout his or her time in S-Anon. At first, this all seemed friendly and supportive. However, since I was new to recovery and had low self-esteem, I felt isolated and left out. My feelings were similar to those I had as a teenager dealing with cliques back when I was in school. Once again, I found myself reluctant to share because I was concerned about what other people might think or say since I had so little experience in the program.

I brought up this issue during a group conscience meeting. I was nervous about sharing my discomfort about these personal references to other members' shares, but my sponsor reminded me that this is part of my experience, strength, and hope. She encouraged me to share my opinion and see what happened. My group was very supportive. The members had not realized that their sharing might be perceived this way. It started a meaningful discussion regarding our group's health in general and the way newcomers are welcomed. Afterward, we all agreed that we grow more personally by being part of a healthy group. After discussions over several weeks, our group agreed to add a reminder to avoid crosstalk before we open the meeting for sharing and to take a group inventory in a few months to reassess how we had been presenting ourselves.

Later, as I worked the Traditions, I learned the importance of unity in S-Anon to ensure that all of our meetings are welcoming to everyone, including newcomers. I try to use my brief sharing time to express my own experience, strength, and hope to the group as a whole and not comment on another person's sharing. That way no one is singled out or left out, and our common welfare is preserved.

• • •

Our group needed a new place to meet. I volunteered to be a member of the "search party" to locate a facility. I found a site where I had a personal connection, knew the rooms well, and felt we would be welcomed. One other member of our group accompanied me to evaluate the potential meeting room, and we agreed it was adequate for our group's needs. When I presented the idea to our S-Anon group, two members expressed their concern that their anonymity and the anonymity of their spouses could be broken, as they knew people outside of the S-Anon program who might be at that location. Since meeting rooms are difficult to come by in our area and my suggestion had not been accepted, I initially felt disappointed and frustrated. I think my ego felt a bit bruised, as well. Our group decided to continue to pray and search for a meeting place that would feel safe and convenient for most of its members. During the process, I realized more fully how important it is to keep our common welfare and unity always in the forefront of our minds. I need to remember that I am not always aware of every point of view. I am grateful when others voice their concerns and provide an opportunity for all of us to better understand a situation.

• • •

Learning about Tradition One has taught me that my thoughts and feelings are just as important as anyone else's. At first I thought that whenever I opened my mouth, I had to sound articulate and insightful. Everyone else's sharing seemed to be so clear and direct. However, I was in so much pain that I could not think clearly and feared that my words would not make sense. Then, at a meeting, someone stated that she was not sure what she would say, but she just needed to share. Once she began, she was eventually able to tell her story. This gave me courage. I began to feel less guarded and self-conscious, so I have been able to share more openly from my heart. I feel more connected to the other members of my group when I let them know who I really am. In the process, I am learning to appreciate more deeply what the word *unity* means.

• • •

Tradition One is teaching me how to make decisions. I grew up in a family where the adults made all the decisions. I did not feel like I had a voice or that I was important. Regarding my own children, I often have made unilateral decisions. Sometimes this is necessary for their safety. However, if I am honest, I could certainly allow them to participate in some decision-making and acknowledge their opinions.

I had an opportunity to put this into practice when we decided to plan a family vacation. In the past, I told the children where we would go and what we would do. Even though I made plans considering what I thought they would enjoy, I realized that this did not give them the feeling that they had a voice. This time we discussed what each of us would like in terms of a vacation. Of course, as the adult, it was my job to include our available time and budget in the planning. One of my daughters asked if we could include a visit to a park with a freshwater spring that she had studied in school. The other children had no particular desire to go there, but they were willing because it was so important to their sister.

By working together, we were able to take a vacation that we all enjoyed, and my daughter's suggestion was one of the highlights! It has become a favorite memory for me. My daughter loved the park, but even more importantly, she said she was glad that we went with her suggestion and proud that she had made a real contribution to our family vacation. My other children learned a valuable lesson about being open and supportive, and I learned a tremendous lesson as well. When I give my children the message that they are important, valuable, and respected, the entire family benefits.

• • •

Using only Conference Approved Literature (CAL) in our meetings supports the common welfare of our members and defines us as S-Anon, apart from any other self-help or study group. A while back, I attended an S-Anon meeting led by a person I respected who had been in the program for a few years. After we

finished the regular CAL, she picked up a non-CAL daily meditation book, which she named and read to us. What did I do? I did
nothing. I did not want to embarrass her in front of the group, and I
assumed she did not realize this was against the Traditions.

After the meeting, I spoke with her and asked if she was aware
that we do not use outside literature. She responded, "Oh, I know
that, but I decided to do it anyway." I was astounded! It seemed to
me that she had purposely violated the suggested guidelines that
define us as a group. I realized that I had an S-Anon slip that day. I
was afraid of embarrassing her and of jeopardizing my own image,
so I did not speak up during the meeting for the common welfare
of the group.

If our common welfare is to come first and we are to avoid outside issues, I must be willing to follow the guidelines and encourage
others to do so, as well. If we do not protect our fellowship, who
will? I am grateful that the S-Anon group was there for me when
I needed it. If it ceases to exist because of our individual fears or
desire to please others, where will those who are still suffering turn
for help in the future?

•   •   •

When I attended my first international convention, I began to
understand a broader meaning of unity in our S-Anon program. My home group is very small, but because we are connected
to the larger fellowship at the Intergroup and international levels,
our S-Anon family is indeed large. At the convention, I felt very
much at home. To see and meet so many fellow travelers on the
road to S-Anon recovery was amazing. When I heard the sharing
at the individual sessions, I was able to see just how far along that
road many members had come. I felt both encouraged and chal-
lenged to take my own progress more seriously. After witnessing
the serenity that others had achieved, I wanted the same for myself.
Until then, I was satisfied with just being familiar with most of the
Steps. I came home determined not to "just be familiar with most of
the Steps," but to actively work the Steps and Traditions with my
sponsor, and to reap the benefits I saw in others. I am beginning to

see how this global unity influences personal progress for all of our members.

• • •

PRACTICING THESE PRINCIPLES

℀

Through working the Steps, we learned to take our focus off the sexaholic and to concentrate on our own recovery instead. After experiencing such freedom, joy, and serenity by doing so, some of us might be hesitant to now include others in our focus. Working the Traditions, however, increases and deepens the recovery that we began by working the S-Anon Twelve Steps. Like the Steps, the Traditions are spiritual principles. They are not rules and they are unenforceable. Rather, they are gentle disciplines that bring us a life of peace.

Tradition One leads us to further growth in our recovery as it encourages us to consider the welfare of the group as well as our own welfare. Our unity is based on a structure that allows for transparency, honesty, and integrity. When we speak to the group, we also are speaking to our Higher Power, so we learn to share with courage and vulnerability. We begin to find our own voice, which is strengthened by sharing at meetings and talking with our sponsors and other S-Anon members.

Tradition One teaches us that our individual welfare depends upon the health of our S-Anon groups and the fellowship as a

The Traditions are boundaries for getting along with others. How pleasant it is to know that, in the fellowship or at home, "our common welfare should come first" instead of the needs and desires of any one person.[2]

---

[2] *Reflections of Hope*, p. 220.

whole. Through the S-Anon program, we pass along the principles of recovery to all of our members, and especially to newcomers. We cannot discern all we need to know about how to recover from the effects of sexaholism on our own; we need a sponsor and each other to guide and encourage us on our S-Anon recovery journey. Our Higher Power speaks to us through others and gives us the tools we need as we work to integrate Tradition One into all areas of our lives.

•   •   •

TRADITION ONE QUESTIONS

Our common welfare should come first;
personal progress for the greatest number
depends upon unity.

1. In my local meetings, do I share my experience, strength, and hope? Do I welcome newcomers and listen to others with an open mind? Do I make program calls between meetings?

2. Do I tend to compare myself to other group members by thinking of myself as being inferior or superior? Do I shy away from or refuse to volunteer for service positions? Do I avoid S-Anon activities except for my meeting?

3. When I share my thoughts and feelings regarding a group concern, do I consider group unity—what is good for the whole—or do I find myself trying to manipulate or control the outcome?

4. Do I share from the S-Anon point of view and keep the focus on my own recovery? Do I tend to use my meetings as a forum to talk about how things ought to be or to complain about the sexaholic or life in general?

5. Do I humble myself, seeking my Higher Power's will, the common welfare of S-Anon, and the unity of my meeting? Do I understand and observe the meeting guidelines for sharing, which include no crosstalk?

6. Do I participate in my group's business meetings, join the discussions, and share my perspective? Do I criticize another member's suggestion, or do I strive for consensus? Do I compare the groups I attend?

7. Am I compassionate toward those with whom I do not agree? Do I make room for other people's opinions? How do I apply Tradition One to relationships outside of my S-Anon group?

8. Am I gentle with myself as well as with others when a difficult situation arises? Am I sometimes stubborn or negative? Do I blame or complain?

9. Am I an informed S-Anon member? Do I take the time to find out what is going on beyond the group level, such as intergroup, World Service Office (WSO), and S-Anon World Service Conferences and Conventions? Do I consider what *common welfare* and *unity* mean at these levels and in all my relationships?

TRADITION TWO

୯୫

*For our group purpose there is but one authority
—a loving God as He may express Himself
in our group conscience. Our leaders are but
trusted servants; they do not govern.*

Tradition Two helps us to make decisions and resolve problems
in our S-Anon groups and in all our other relationships. Just as
the first three Steps guide us to turn our individual lives over to
the care of God, Tradition Two invites us to do the same in all our
interactions. We can admit our powerlessness and acknowledge
that we may not have all the answers. We start to place our trust in
our Higher Power and the wisdom expressed through each member
of the group and begin to let go of the outcomes. When we put our
common welfare first, we surrender our self-will and allow God
to guide us in making group decisions that both honor our own
recovery and support S-Anon's primary purpose: to help families
and friends of sexaholics.

For many of us, this spiritual approach to life may be new.
Group decision-making, as well as the group's meeting format,
might have seemed confusing when we first came to S-Anon. While
various members facilitated the meetings, there did not seem to be
an official "leader" of the group. No one seemed to be "in charge,"
and no one individual made decisions for the group. Instead, in
S-Anon, a group of people with different backgrounds and personalities worked together as equals to consider various points of view
and make decisions. This may have been the first time we heard a
group ask a Higher Power to guide members in setting priorities
without controlling others or being controlled. As newcomers,
many of us may have been impressed by such a humble and democratic approach.

Just as we make personal decisions based on our individual conscience, we make group decisions in S-Anon based on the collective conscience of the members present. We call this group decision-making taking a *group conscience*. We ask our Higher Power to guide this process and direct our decisions. As we address each issue, we try to balance our personal preferences with the good of our group as a whole. We each have an opportunity to voice our opinions. We serve the group by sharing our opinions honestly, even if they differ from those of other members. We have learned through our experience that it is important to listen and consider all opinions. The opinion of someone at his or her first meeting may be just as helpful to the group as that of a long-time member. When each member speaks, we may hear new ideas or principles that could positively influence the group's decision. A loving God speaks through all of us, and as we consider the opinions of others, we may change our point of view. We want to be open to what our Higher Power is trying to say to us. Our willingness to be humble in decision-making is key to maintaining the health and unity of our group. Once all members have had a chance to share and discuss different options, the group votes on the issues and comes to a decision. Some groups abide by majority rule, and others work toward consensus. Sometimes the particular issue determines the approach used.

Some examples of subjects for a group conscience are which meeting topics to cover each week, how to reach out to newcomers, and how to fill service positions. For some decisions, such as determining a new meeting location, we obtain as much information as possible beforehand.

We may discuss certain issues at more than one group conscience meeting to ensure all group members have had ample time to consider them and form an opinion. We try to avoid procrastination or indecision by using a realistic timeframe to come to a group decision. Giving careful, thorough consideration to decisions allows us time and opportunity to seek our Higher Power's guiding voice. Participation in a group conscience helps us understand that this process actually does work; we are part of a group where our individual opinions matter and where we can be heard and valued.

Before we came to S-Anon, many of us struggled with trust and control. As stated in the S-Anon Problem, "We chose friends and partners who could not or would not love and support us in a healthy way."[3] Some of us reacted to sexaholism by attempting to control everything we could. We made all of the decisions in our lives without consulting anyone else. Others handed over the decision-making to the sexaholic or others and then felt resentful when things did not turn out to our liking. Neither approach helped us feel valued, accepted, or understood. In S-Anon we gain courage to speak up, eventually coming to believe that we have a voice and a point of view with merit, whether or not we agree with the final decision. As a fellowship of equals, we benefit from sharing our views with all in attendance during the group conscience meeting rather than forming factions by promoting our ideas in small groups or cliques. We focus on "principles above personalities," respect confidentiality, and refrain from gossip. Taking a group conscience helps us learn to make decisions with integrity and respect.

Decisions we make as a group may not be perfect, but when each member strives to follow Tradition Two, we can trust that the decision is the one we are meant to reach today. We may not always see the big picture, but we trust that our Higher Power does. Sometimes, especially if the process does not include hearing all sides of the issue or does not include humbly listening to God's guidance, we may make decisions that are not beneficial to our group. Other decisions may appear advantageous at the time but require reconsideration when circumstances change. We learn to be flexible and make necessary adjustments when more is revealed to us.

When we say in Tradition Two, "Our leaders are but trusted servants...," it means that we can humbly put our trust in our Higher Power to guide those in leadership positions. We set our egos aside. We serve in various capacities and roles in order to support the purposes and goals of the group as a whole. We serve in a transparent and honest way, without expecting praise or special

------

[3] *Working the S-Anon Program,* p. 125.

recognition. As leaders, we offer support and encouragement rather than trying to force our will on others by manipulating, dictating, repeating, or commanding.

Humility in service is the key difference between governing and leading. Governing implies that there are various rules that someone has the power to determine and enforce. When we try to govern in S-Anon, we may think we know what is best for another person or for our group. Step One reminds us that we are truly powerless over others, and any action that intimidates or bullies other members under the guise of being helpful is not consistent with humility.

In contrast, when we lead, we turn others over to the care of their own Higher Power so we can focus on ourselves and respect each other as equals. We offer suggestions from our own experience, strength, and hope; and follow the Twelve Traditions and other S-Anon spiritual principles to the best of our ability. We learn to ask for help when we need it. Leading provides us an opportunity to improve our self-esteem and helps us to build trust in God, in ourselves, and in other members.

The idea of "trusted servant" offers guidance to our groups as well. Just as our leaders do not dictate, neither do we attempt to tell them how to fulfill their roles. Learning to let go of control and to trust appropriately are two benefits of the S-Anon program. We have an opportunity to practice these as we work together with our trusted servants. As members, we may provide help when asked, but we still trust our leaders to do their jobs as they think best.

A trusted servant can be any member of our program; there are no requirements for service at the group level. Some groups may have suggestions for length of time in the program or level of Step work completed, but these are not requirements. In order to keep this a fellowship of equals, we step out of a service position after a set period so that no one person becomes the "authority." When we find a way to balance responsibility and humility, we become accountable and reliable leaders. We neither have to be prodded to serve, nor do we take over and dominate others. We show up with the willingness to serve; we do only our part and trust that our Higher Power will guide our service and take care of everyone and everything else.

As we grow in our understanding of Tradition Two, we can learn to use these same principles in our personal and professional lives. We see how important it is for us to take as much time as necessary before making decisions. We invite our Higher Power into the process and pray for guidance. When we make decisions as individuals, we can gather support by asking the opinion of others in our lives, such as our sponsor, other S-Anon members, and trusted family or friends. When we make decisions with the people in our families, at our workplaces, and in all our other groups, we learn to listen with respect to the opinions of others. We consider all sides of an issue. For instance, our families may have meetings where we invite every person to share an opinion, just as we do in S-Anon. Even our children are able to have a voice. As we become more aware that everyone's opinion has value, we can let go of trying to control the outcome.

S-Anon seeks to provide a safe place to practice the attitudes and skills we want to employ in all aspects of our lives. Over time, we will begin to find the balance between giving and receiving in our relationships with others. With the help of our Higher Power, we will become able to participate in S-Anon service and group decision-making with humility, seeking to respect and encourage others and ourselves.

• • •

Tradition Two has helped me to trust that I can express my thoughts and opinions without fear. As a newcomer, I observed how the group members made decisions and worked through problems in a way that was fair to everyone, without  yelling or giving each other the silent treatment. This was something new to me. They spoke up and gave their opinions and were still loved and accepted. I learned that I, too, could speak up and still feel safe.

This kind of trust has been more difficult to build in my relationship with the sexaholic. When we disagree, I fear the sexaholic will no longer love me or will turn against me. When I was a child, I learned that disagreement led to criticism and rejection. I was afraid to speak up, and it took a while for me to try it in my S-Anon group. I was relieved to find that I was not criticized or rejected. In fact, some people in the group actually thanked me for saying what I said. In my relationships, I often find myself trying to either please or control. I am learning this is far more harmful to me and to our relationship than I had ever imagined!

In S-Anon, I am discovering how to respect myself. I want to be an equal and sane participant in all of my relationships more than I want to be "right." My opinions and feelings are valid. I am learning to keep the focus on myself and to let go of my obsession with what other people might be thinking of me. I try to examine my motives before I speak. I can ask my Higher Power to guide me and give me courage as I strive to be authentic in all my relationships.

• • •

I had been in recovery for about a year and still felt like a newcomer. My sponsor recommended I seek out and attend additional meetings and urged me to continue speaking up for my needs. I was becoming more aware of my feelings, and I knew the opportunity to practice what I learned was in my best interest. I needed to commit to my recovery and go to any lengths to further it. I had to become willing to speak up if something was bothering me, even though that was very frightening to me.

Despite my fear, I found an additional meeting. The leader opened the meeting and immediately began directing the group on how it works and who does what, when, and how. The leader also gave feedback, advice, and encouragement to members after their shares. Not only did I consider it cross talk, but I thought she had set herself as the governor and authority of the S-Anon group. I felt uncomfortable and controlled. I did not feel safe and wanted to run out the door as quickly as possible, but I knew I needed to speak up and ask for what I needed before I left. I did not know exactly what to say, so I asked my Higher Power to give me the words I needed to address the issue. After everyone shared, I asked if I could say something before the meeting closed. I said I felt uncomfortable with crosstalk during the meeting and with the leader giving feedback and advice to members after they shared. I made reference to Tradition Two, which tells us our leaders are trusted servants, but they do not govern the meetings.

I am so glad I can now recognize the value of the Traditions and speak up to support them. S-Anon is a safe place where I can go to discuss my problems and find a solution—a place to learn and to grow and to practice what I learn. To ensure that I continue to have a safe place to go for recovery, I will speak up for Tradition Two and practice it as best as I can.

• • •

When I began to understand that if I wanted to keep what I had been given in S-Anon, I had to give it away, I started to appreciate the exceptional value of doing service. I believe my Higher Power encouraged my good intentions and my strong feelings of gratitude for the S-Anon program. I was becoming more honest with myself about my motives. I did not want to overextend myself, and yet I did want to volunteer to serve. I accepted a service position, and most of the time I did pretty well. I found that I wanted to fulfill my commitments in a timely manner, encourage other members, and cooperate with them in our service work. I saw how our working together helped the group be there for me and for others. Because service in S-Anon counteracts my tendencies to be self-absorbed and to isolate, it is helping me to grow up. It has been very rewarding for me.

• • •

I volunteered to help my group prepare for a local recovery retreat by making copies of the paperwork that each member would receive that day. I chose to use my home copier, as I was not comfortable making copies at the local business where I frequently made copies for another organization. I was concerned about my anonymity should anyone happen to walk by and notice the name S-Anon or the content. Some members of my group objected to this because they thought the group would not be "fully self-supporting" (Tradition Seven) if I made the copies at home and donated them. We talked about it. In the discussion, I mentioned that as a *trusted servant*, I hoped that they would trust me to do the job as I saw fit without sacrificing my anonymity. We were able to resolve the conflict by having the group reimburse me for the cost of the paper and ink involved. I appreciate that we were able to voice our opinions, consider how to best honor the Traditions, and reach a compromise that satisfied all our concerns.

• • •

Helping out after the birth of a second grandchild is giving me a new appreciation of the value of Tradition Two. Through the gifts of the program, my style of "helping" has changed from authority to trusted servant. I participate in decisions by offering my thoughts and then letting go of the outcome. My daughter often asks my opinion, and I also offer it on my own when I think it might be of value, but I can now offer my experience as one way of doing things rather than as the only right way. I frequently comment, "This is my vote on the issue, but of course it is your decision." I think my daughter appreciates this more considerate and less bossy attitude. I am here to serve and support, not to control and dictate. I ask my Higher Power to help me remember that and to guide my interactions. I am learning to say things like, "Is now a good time for me to give the baby his bath?" rather than, "I am going to give the baby his bath now." I try to gently remind my daughter of her doctor's instructions not to pick up anything heavier than the baby right now, rather than just insisting she let me carry the diaper bag. This kinder, humbler, gentler approach is more respectful to my daughter and helps to create an atmosphere of peace and harmony. I still make mistakes and slip into an authoritarian mode, but I am quicker to recognize that now and make amends. Tension can build more quickly since we are sleep-deprived, so timely amends are especially important. Having a new baby in the family is both joyous and stressful, but applying Tradition Two has lessened the stress and increased the joy. I am so grateful.

• • •

PRACTICING
THESE
PRINCIPLES

❧

Our service in S-Anon begins when we show up at meetings and honestly share our experience, strength, and hope. Even listening to others share is a service that benefits all of us. When we eventually take the risk of investing in ourselves by taking on additional responsibilities as trusted servants, our personal recovery grows even more. Our sense of loyalty and belonging grows deeper as we work together and become a vital part of something bigger than ourselves.

> *Working this program has allowed me to make progress in clearly speaking my opinion and letting Higher Power guide the outcome.*[4]

Working together is not always easy. Making decisions together sometimes may bring out our defects of character; we are not perfect. We may struggle with a desire to control outcomes, promote our own ideas, manipulate others, or withhold our opinions. We may experience fear, resentment, or even indifference when we need to make a particular decision with others. We might recognize that we can be self-centered and only want to consider our own point of view. The desire to feel "right" or justified in our thoughts or actions may lead us to view ourselves as better than other members. We may have trouble letting go and accepting decisions that do not align with our own personal views. Working Step Ten by taking a personal inventory regarding our part in the decision-making process can reveal defects of character that may be hindering us. Doing service in S-Anon will

---

[4] *Reflections of Hope,* p. 260.

provide us with opportunities to recognize these defects, surrender them to our Higher Power, and grow in our recovery.

We remember that different opinions can be useful and are not personal criticisms, even though we may feel defensive or justified in our stance. We can invite our Higher Power to help us reach the best solution. When we let go of outcomes, our burdens are lifted.

Sometimes, we might disagree with the group's decision. We can feel uncomfortable, disappointed, or even betrayed when we experience any discord with the very group that has been the source of such help, comfort, and serenity for us. Despite understanding that dignity and self-worth are part of the journey of recovery, our self-esteem may still be fragile. Perhaps some of our old ways of dealing with sexaholism, such as obsession, isolation, withdrawal, and rage, may resurface.

We now have another option: we can apply the new tools that we discover in S-Anon to deal with the issue at hand. We can pause and consider how to respond rather than react. Many of us have found it helpful to reflect with a sponsor or other program member about the feelings and thoughts associated with our situation. Our literature has many references to group conscience, so reading and contemplating the wisdom available to us through this tool can be helpful. We can also move toward serenity when we apply slogans such as "Easy Does It," write about our feelings in our journal, and meditate on the Serenity Prayer.

With the help of our Higher Power and the application of the spiritual principles of the S-Anon program, we come to recognize the value of observing Tradition Two. We appreciate its wisdom in creating a fellowship of equals with our only authority being a loving God of our understanding, and we are grateful for the guidance and serenity that it imparts to us, to our group, and to our fellowship, one day at a time.

• • •

TRADITION TWO QUESTIONS

For our group purpose there is but one authority—a loving God as He may express Himself in our group conscience. Our leaders are but trusted servants; they do not govern.

1. How do I consult my Higher Power before I speak? Is what I am about to say thoughtful, helpful, intelligent, necessary, and kind? (T.H.I.N.K.) In what way do I show my understanding that we are a fellowship of equals?

2. If I think there is something that my group needs to discuss, do I ask for a group conscience? Do I avoid creating cliques or factions by not gossiping about the issue with a few members?

3. How do I support the group decision-making process by being informed and prepared? Am I patient with the time needed for the group to work through an issue?

4. At group conscience meetings, do I listen respectfully when others share their opinions, even if I disagree? Do I speak up and share my views honestly and thoughtfully, yet without dominating the discussion? Am I open to changing my opinion after considering all other opinions? Am I able to compromise rather than insist that things go my way?

5. Do I accept the decision as the voice of our Higher Power speaking through the group members? Do I respond rather than react if it goes against the way I think things ought to be? Do I use the tools of the program to help me if I am having difficulty?

6. How do I understand our group purpose? Who acts as the primary authority in my S-Anon group? In my work? In my family? How can I invite my Higher Power's presence into these relationships?

7. In what ways do I show support for the members who fill service positions? Do I express my gratitude to them for their service? Do I avoid criticizing? Do I offer my experience if asked, yet allow them to do the job as they see fit?

8. How am I willing to serve the group? Do I recognize that my group is made possible by the larger fellowship of S-Anon, and that there are service opportunities and needs beyond the group level? Am I able to serve the fellowship in any of these ways? What particular gifts and talents do I have (or want to develop) that would help me serve in particular positions? Have I discussed possible service opportunities with my sponsor?

9. When I accept a service position, do I perform it to the best of my ability? Do I willingly give up service positions when the commitment time is over? What has been the result?

10. When making family decisions, do I take time to listen to everyone's opinion, even those of the youngest members of the family? Do I express my opinions clearly and respectfully? What has been my experience in family decisions?

11. Do I try to "keep the peace at any price" because I am uncomfortable with conflict? Or do I practice the principles of Tradition Two and express my opinion in a healthy way?

TRADITION THREE

The relatives of sexaholics, when gathered together for mutual aid, may call themselves an S-Anon family group, provided that, as a group, they have no other affiliation. The only requirement for membership is that there be a problem of sexaholism in a relative or friend.

Recovering from serious loss, trauma, or addiction is difficult to do alone. Just as sexaholics may seek recovery with other sexaholics, their family members and friends can also benefit from joining together in recovery. Finding others who have been affected by someone else's sex addiction and who are willing to listen and share their experience, strength, and hope can be a great relief. With the help of our Higher Power, our S-Anon Family Groups are able to offer a safe haven of mutual support and compassionate understanding.

We may think that our problems are unique, and we may feel that we are alone in this situation, but in S-Anon we soon discover that we have much in common with other members. We recognize that even though the exact details of sexaholism in our lives may differ, the effects upon us are much the same. When we face our problems together in a safe environment with others who understand, the power the disease has over us lessens with time. Experiencing acceptance and love from other members offers us hope and encouragement as we begin our recovery.

We each decide for ourselves if we belong in S-Anon. The only requirement for membership is that there be a problem of sexaholism in a relative or friend. We qualify for S-Anon because someone's sexual behavior concerns us. Our personal philosophy, political views, education, profession, economic status, sexual orientation, race, and religious background are not relevant, nor do we mention these in S-Anon meetings. We welcome and accept all who have been affected by sexaholism. It is not necessary that the sexaholic acknowledge his or her disease or be in recovery for us to seek help for ourselves in S-Anon.

Occasionally, sexaholics may realize that they have been affected by the sexaholism of another person, and therefore they also qualify for S-Anon. We offer them the same welcome and compassion that we give to all new members.

We want to be available to all who are suffering, so some local areas have an S-Anon contact phone line for individuals to call for information about S-Anon. Generally, the caller leaves a message. A local member returns the call, asks why the caller is seeking S-Anon, and offers a warm and compassionate welcome. The member can explain the one requirement for membership, what to expect during a meeting, and the meeting times and locations. He or she can offer an empathetic ear and answer any questions. No matter how our first contact with an S-Anon member occurred, we know the importance of being welcomed and offered understanding, encouragement, and hope.

Our goal is to offer a sense of belonging and equality for everyone. During our meetings, we speak only from the S-Anon point of view. We keep our focus on ourselves and our own recovery. We share how our thinking, attitudes, and behavior have been affected by the disease of sexaholism. We also share the positive changes we are making in our lives through working the S-Anon program. We avoid gossiping, comparing ourselves to others, and making demeaning remarks about the sexaholic. We only refer to and use S-Anon Conference Approved Literature. Those of us who participate in other Twelve-Step programs do not talk about them. We also avoid mentioning any specific therapist, treatment program, book, or author, as well as our religion, profession, and other affiliations or organizations. However, outside of our meeting times we can talk about whatever we wish.

As individuals, we may seek whatever support or spiritual comfort we want or need in addition to the S-Anon program, but we do not mention this during a meeting. We acknowledge that there are many other paths to recovery, beneficial causes, and worthwhile endeavors. However, our experience shows us that we dilute the benefits of S-Anon when we stray from our primary purpose: to offer help and support to families and friends of sexaholics. We cannot be all things to all people, so we focus on our program principles during our meetings. We do not advertise or sell products, services, or philosophies, nor do we solicit help either with or from any outside enterprise. Engaging in these activities could be interpreted as affiliation and divert us from our primary spiritual aim. Furthermore, when we choose the name of our group, we do not include the name of the facility where we meet in order to prevent any reference that might indicate an affiliation.

If a member does not observe the meeting guidelines, we may gently restate them during the meeting or explain them privately afterwards. To keep our meetings healthy, we try to ensure that nothing jeopardizes our common goal of recovery. Staying focused on our primary purpose also helps us avoid controversy that could threaten the group's unity and become an obstacle to our recovery. Our meetings are relatively short, and some people drive long distances for the help that S-Anon offers. We want to make wise use of our time together, so we try to keep the focus on why we are here.

When we gather together for mutual aid, we help ourselves and other members whose lives have been affected by another person's sexual addiction. Time, regular attendance at meetings, and working the S-Anon program can help us overcome long-standing negative patterns and adopt healthier attitudes. Eventually we begin to feel *a part of* rather than *apart from*. When we apply the tools of the S-Anon program, one day at a time, we will begin to see the gifts of recovery, including fellowship, serenity, and joy. With the help of our Higher Power, we discover new ways of thinking and learn to respond rather than react. We enhance our personal recovery by practicing these new skills with fellow members. Our strength is rooted in our shared goal, which helps us to maintain a unified focus.

We can apply the same welcoming spirit of Tradition Three to other parts of our lives as well. Having experienced the importance of a sense of belonging, we grow in our desire to convey this same acceptance, understanding, and encouragement to others, no matter where we are. We learn to focus on what unites us rather than on what divides us. Whether in relationships with fellow group members or with other people in our lives, we can experience the generous, open-minded attitude fostered by Tradition Three while still maintaining our personal integrity and the health of our group.

•   •   •

I remember sitting quietly and listening as my sexaholic partner told me about S-Anon, a program that could help me. On the outside I was courteous, while on the inside I felt like I wanted to explode. I could see this was terribly important to him;

Tradition Three
STORIES

however, it turned out to be vital for me as well. When he finished explaining, he handed me a piece of paper with the S-Anon contact information.

The first thing I did was to call my current sponsor from another Twelve Step program. Much to my surprise, she told me a part of her story I had never heard before. She had been married to a sexaholic years before. She was well acquainted with Twelve Step programs, so after discovering his disease, she had looked for help. S-Anon was not in existence, so, regrettably, there was no one to welcome her and show her that she was not alone in the problem.

After our phone conversation, I called the S-Anon helpline in my area. I received a call back from a local S-Anon member. She listened quietly and respectfully as I shared my feelings of fear and discomfort. She helped me to understand that I could benefit from S-Anon because of my relationship with a sexaholic. She gave me information about the meetings and suggested that I attend one near my home the following night.

I know now this was Tradition Three in action. I am grateful that the wisdom found in Tradition Three helps me today when I take calls from people who are affected by someone's sex addiction.

• • •

The first S-Anon meeting I attended was in 1986, when S-Anon was only in its third year. I arrived early and found four women seated on tiny kiddie chairs and huddled around a kindergarten-size table.

They were few in number and very grateful for newcomers. They seemed genuinely happy to see me and asked me to join them. They explained that they were writing a draft about the S-Anon Steps. I was surprised when they asked me to share my experience, strength, and hope. They invited me to write with them, and so I did. They were a small group coming together every Saturday night before the regular meeting time. They understood the need to have S-Anon stories told in print so that many more people could identify with the writing and learn where to go for help.

My experience with those four women in those tiny little chairs became the foundation of my understanding of what is meant in Tradition Three, "...we gather together for mutual aid." I gained a great sense of belonging when they asked me to join them in their labor of love. The work we did would eventually contribute to our book, *S-Anon Twelve Steps*.

• • •

When a newcomer shared that she was not only in need of help for her problems involving a sexaholic, but also that she herself had a sexual addiction, I became somewhat anxious. When she spoke of her frustration because she could not control the sexaholic, I was able to relate to that. However, when she started to describe her sexaholic feelings and actions, I knew right away why we have Tradition Three to help guide our meetings. Her comments tended to steer the meeting off course and triggered uncomfortable and critical thoughts in me. The other members became very quiet. I waited until after the meeting to gently speak with her in a non-shaming way. I told her that she was welcome in S-Anon and that I hoped she would keep coming back. I reminded her of our guidelines about sharing only from the S-Anon point of view. She apologized and thanked me for bringing that to her attention.

• • •

Early in my recovery, I was seeing a counselor as well as attending S-Anon meetings. I recall during one meeting, I enthusiastically began to describe to my fellow S-Anon members a workshop my counselor had recommended. Because this workshop also dealt with recovery from the effects of sexaholism, I thought that my sharing about it would be helpful to others. I did not recognize that I was diluting the S-Anon message by using our meeting time to discuss a different approach to recovery. I was unfamiliar with Tradition Three, so I was somewhat chagrined and embarrassed when one of the more experienced members gently asked me to save any comments like that until the meeting was over. As I have grown in my understanding of the S-Anon program and Traditions, I have become increasingly grateful for her reminder. During a meeting, I do not want to distract others or myself from the S-Anon point of view.

●   ●   ●

PRACTICING
THESE
PRINCIPLES

ॐ

A s S-Anon members, we offer a warm welcome to all members, whether they attend regularly after their first meeting or return to the program after many years. We can encourage newcomers to "keep coming back," but we do not pressure them. We accept God's timing and avoid the faulty thinking that we can control others and outcomes. We are all welcome to take what we like from our meetings and leave the rest.

The spiritual principle in Tradition Three asks us to maintain a sense of belonging and equality for everyone.[5]

We learn to practice the principles of Tradition Three in every area of our lives. Two common effects upon us of another person's sexaholism are that we may easily lapse into judgmental thinking and jump to conclusions. Tradition Three can help us avoid making snap judgments about people and assumptions about circumstances. It reminds us to develop a welcoming spirit and to appreciate our differences, while still maintaining healthy boundaries.

We recognize that before recovery, we might have placed unhealthy "membership requirements" on our friends, relatives, and other people in our lives, wanting them to meet all our expectations. Perhaps we criticized others for some of their choices, rather than respecting their individuality and accepting them for who they were. Perhaps we thought that to be in a relationship with us, other people had to agree with all of our opinions, do things our way, and view life from our perspective. Having unrealistic expectations and

---

[5] *Working the S-Anon Program*, p. 31.

judgmental attitudes may have prevented us from experiencing some mutually beneficial and enriching relationships.

As we begin to adopt the principles of Tradition Three, we find ourselves becoming less controlling, less critical of others, and less sure that we know what others are thinking. With the help of our Higher Power, we grow more tolerant, hospitable, and considerate of others as we focus on what is important in our own lives and recovery. S-Anon offers a spiritual way to ease our suffering and helps us learn how to live fuller and more peaceful lives.

●　　●　　●

TRADITION THREE QUESTIONS

The relatives of sexaholics, when gathered together for mutual aid, may call themselves an S-Anon Family Group, provided that, as a group, they have no other affiliation. The only requirement for membership is that there be a problem of sexaholism in a relative or friend.

1. How do I help create a safe and welcoming place for all newcomers, even if they differ from me in age, gender, sexual orientation, religion, education, ethnicity, or socioeconomic background? Do I make judgments about who belongs and who does not belong in an S-Anon meeting?

2. How can my group welcome members of other Twelve-Step programs and yet maintain the S-Anon point of view? Why is it important to leave other Twelve-Step issues outside of the meeting?

3. How can I treat others and myself in ways that show acceptance, tolerance and love?

4. How does my group encourage sharing from all members? How does my group accept those who do not wish to share?

5. Do I support the primary purpose of S-Anon? Am I inclined to promote or discuss outside issues during the meeting? Do I understand how this can dilute the S-Anon message? What impact does veering from our primary purpose have on me and other members, especially newcomers?

6. How can I remain open to new ideas and yet ensure that my group does not affiliate with any outside cause or organization? How can my group guard against the dilution of the S-Anon message?

7. Is it clear that the place where our group meets has no affiliation with our group?

8. Do I create requirements for S-Anon membership in my head? For example, do I think that membership should be limited to those who are always on time, attend meetings regularly, and do service? Or maybe to just those who have been affected by the sexaholism of a spouse or partner?

TRADITION FOUR

❧

*Each group should be autonomous, except in
matters affecting another group or S-Anon
or SA as a whole.*

In S-Anon we need both independence and unity to flourish. With
our Higher Power's help, we strive for a healthy balance between
the two. Tradition Four offers guidance to our groups by stress-
ing the importance of the autonomy of each group as well as our
responsibility to consider how that autonomy affects others.

Autonomy is an important S-Anon principle that offers freedom from external control. It encourages us to determine our own
course regarding our group matters and our own concerns. S-Anon
Family Groups have the right to be autonomous when we make
decisions about what works best within S-Anon guidelines and
principles. Autonomy makes it possible for our groups to learn and
mature at our own pace by giving us the opportunity to make mistakes and learn from them. This allows for flexibility when we need
to make changes. Each group develops its own unique personality
and decides how to best respond to members' needs. We maintain
the S-Anon point of view, yet, as a group, we have the freedom to
select such things as meeting focus and topics; prayers and read-
ings that appear in our Conference Approved Literature; speakers;
Seventh Tradition allocations; how and when to have a business
meeting and hold a group conscience; ways to reach out to potential
S-Anon members; and how to help newcomers.

With such freedom comes responsibility. Another definition
of autonomy is "self-governing," which implies that we learn to
place limits on ourselves. Our autonomy is guided by the principle
of being responsible to the worldwide fellowship. Tradition Four

encourages us to take into account what is good for S-Anon as a whole. Individuals, groups, Intergroups, Areas, and Regions are cautioned to guard against making decisions that would adversely affect another group or present an inaccurate or unfavorable picture of the S-Anon program. We are the face of S-Anon; if we convey a negative impression, we could discourage newcomers, cause confusion, or create controversy.

Careful consideration of the potential impact of a decision on the entire fellowship is vital to our unity. While Tradition Four, like the other Traditions, is not a rule and is not enforceable, it is fundamental to the health of S-Anon. We are not asked to be obedient to a rule, but rather, to be obedient to the unenforceable. Therefore, we try to follow these important guidelines willingly because experience has shown that they are necessary to protect the unity of our fellowship.

It is essential that each meeting be based upon well-established S-Anon principles. For example, we only use S-Anon Conference Approved Literature (CAL) during our meetings. This assures that the focus of our meetings remains based on S-Anon principles. If a group does not abide by Tradition Four, it may be because members are not aware of it. Members who are familiar with Tradition Four have a responsibility to speak up and share their experience, strength, and hope to gently educate newcomers and remind others when necessary. We cannot control outcomes, but we can share what we have learned.

As individuals, fellow workers, and family members, Tradition Four helps guide our attitudes and resulting behaviors. We can learn to interact in a healthier way simply by observing what happens at S-Anon meetings that abide by Tradition Four. Part of our recovery may include recognizing and accepting that we have needs, wants, and opinions. We can learn to express them and accept that people may agree or disagree. We begin to show consideration more easily to others and ourselves, and we become better able to treat everyone with courtesy, honesty, and respect. As we develop a deep sense of the freedom of our personal autonomy, we come to understand that others also have the right to their autonomy. We grow in awareness that what they do is not our business except in matters that affect us directly or that affect those for whom we are responsible.

Tradition Four also helps us when we make decisions by encouraging us to consider how those decisions might impact our family, friends, co-workers, or other people in our lives. We do not want to discount our own needs, but at the same time, we do want to consider the needs of others. We treat them and ourselves with courtesy and honesty and try to listen to and follow the guidance of our Higher Power. By doing so, we develop and accept limits within our autonomy and take responsibility for our actions and reactions.

When we seek help from a Higher Power, we grow in our understanding of how to live in harmony with other people as well as with ourselves. Learning to act not only with autonomy but also with consideration of others is a vital skill that improves all areas of our lives.

•   •   •

I did not know what to expect when I attended my first International Convention. Since I grew up in a chaotic and unpredictable family, I especially appreciated the consistency and reliability I experienced in my S-Anon meeting. My sponsor encouraged me

to attend the convention, but I felt anxious about leaving the safe cocoon of my local meeting. What if there was a guest speaker who distracted me from my recovery, or what if I attended a meeting where someone decided to make changes to the Twelve Steps? I was worried that something might happen that would negatively affect the sense of security and safety I had found in S-Anon. As it turned out, nothing like that occurred, and the convention was a great boost to my recovery.

At the time, I was relatively new in the program and did not yet understand how Tradition Four helps safeguard our fellowship. Now that I am aware of how it helps guide our trusted servants who plan S-Anon events, I can feel more assured that the message of S-Anon will be conveyed clearly. My S-Anon recovery is helping me to participate more fully and even to contribute to the safety and consistency of the program.

•   •   •

I have spent a great deal of time either being too focused on unity or acting with too much independence. My S-Anon problem manifested itself in both ways. In unbalanced unity, I abandoned myself for the benefit of another or for a group. In unbalanced independence, I isolated and became so self-reliant that I ignored the needs of others. I have learned from Tradition Four that I can be true to myself without cutting myself off from others.

I often chose to become entirely autonomous. I frequently thought that others were either with me or against me. I took someone else's decision personally, especially if it was the opposite of what I wanted. Then I was either angry and upset or terrified and lonely. None of those feelings was a healthy basis on which to make a decision or take action. This is where I can turn to Tradition Four for guidance.

How many times have my actions or inactions negatively affected others? Far more often than I would like. How many times have I invited my Higher Power to guide my actions? Not often enough. Since coming to S-Anon, I am able to get spiritual guidance by going to God first and asking for help with my decisions and actions.

Tradition Four, like the other Traditions, is a powerful tool. It teaches me about the delicate balance between unity and freedom. I experience peace of mind and release from the bondage of self when I act on my own behalf without harming others.

• • •

For me, the most difficult part of trying to live the spirit of Tradition Four (balancing independence and harmony) has been communicating with and considering others as part of my decision-making process. Part of my pre-recovery thinking was that I had to do everything myself and that I knew best.

I ran into trouble by becoming too busy to recognize my own feelings or to be aware of the feelings of the people around me. I had this great big never-ending "To Do" list in my head that needed to be completed now, and I believed that everyone in my family should help me with it. In my attempt to accomplish what I thought needed to get done, I often ignored the "consider how this affects others" principle that is an important part of Tradition Four. I became totally autonomous. I now can see how I didn't stop to think about harmony at all, other than whether or not others were in harmony with my plan. I didn't ask, and I often didn't slow down long enough to update those impacted by my Big Important Plan. In my tunnel vision, I pushed my agenda in order to make sure things went the way I wanted.

This felt normal to me because of my experience in my family of origin. My independence affected my family just as my mother's affected me. I now recognize that I can act on my choices for myself only until they impact the rest of the family. I am learning to ask the question, "Will this decision affect others?" If so, I can slow down and discuss my ideas and try to work out an agreeable solution. Tradition Four is helping to create more harmony in my family.

• • •

Without asking ahead of time, I committed my spouse to participate in a community activity with me. I could see by the frustrated and annoyed response I got that I had crossed the line into inconsiderate behavior.

This was part of an old pattern of mine, so at our next meeting, my sponsor reminded me of Tradition Four and suggested that I ask those involved beforehand how they feel about my plans. I claimed that I meant to ask but just forgot. But, did I really mean to ask? I realized that I had not even thought of my spouse's part in the equation.

I have to admit, there have been many times my well-intentioned plans have upset or inconvenienced others. Perhaps my agenda has become my Higher Power. With help from my sponsor, I am beginning to see how powerless I am over this struggle. While I deeply crave connection with others, I do not attract it when I act independently and without consideration. I now do a nightly Tenth Step inventory around my "out of balance autonomy," which I am finding to be really helpful.

I have come to appreciate both the simplicity and complexity of Tradition Four, and I am completely humbled by how difficult it has been to apply it to my life. The Traditions are often challenging and eye-opening concepts for me. They take my Fourth Step work and deepen it. I can see that God has a lot to teach me through studying them.

• • •

I have found Tradition Four to be very beneficial during the S-Anon Delegate meetings. On the monthly calls, the delegates discuss various topics, such as ways to help newcomers. There is no one "right" way to welcome newcomers and introduce them to the S-Anon program. Our groups have autonomy in this area, so we are free to make our own decisions as long as our actions do not harm other groups or S-Anon as a whole. During the delegate discussions, no one suggests that we all have to approach this issue the same way; we simply share the ideas that have worked in our area. For example, one idea was to invite newcomers to step outside the meeting for a few minutes to meet one-on-one with a current member. Another idea was to put a card on the table that further clarified the meeting guidelines for newcomers and current members alike. Through this sharing, we are able to bring new ideas back to our groups, who then have the freedom to decide if they wish to try them.

•   •   •

PRACTICING
THESE
PRINCIPLES

୬୧

Tradition Four is a spiritual principle that can lead us to peace and harmony, but it may take time to learn how to incorporate it into our lives. It begins by acknowledging that each group, each individual, has the right to be autonomous. At first, it may seem to imply that we can do what we want, but the other side of this Tradition reveals that this is not entirely the case. Tradition Four is about exercising individuality in harmony with others. It is about a creating a balance between unity and independence, which is not easy. Finding the equilibrium between the two strengthens us as individuals, our relationships with others, and our fellowship as a whole.

Tradition Four reminds us to consider how the actions of our group may affect others as we participate in meetings and other S-Anon activities. Tradition Four can also guide our family relationships....[6]

When exercising autonomy, we have a responsibility to look at ourselves and be mindful of controlling behavior that could destroy the group as well as our other relationships. We try to remember that our spiritual illness (our S-Anon Problem) can cause faulty thinking, such as believing that we know what is best for other people, insisting loudly and repeatedly that the group follow one person's recommendations, or assuming that we know what other people are thinking. Our perceptions are not always reality.

---

[6] *Working the S-Anon Program,* pp. 31 & 32.

In S-Anon recovery, we try to keep an open mind, and we ask our Higher Power to help us see and embrace reality.

Because of our spiritual illness, we can be triggered into behaving the way we always did. Conflict can arise when we try to force our personal agenda without considering how it affects everyone involved. We now have our S-Anon group, CAL, and our Higher Power to help us see what reasonable behavior looks like. By exercising humility, we are better able to see where we are wrong, correct it, and make amends. We remember the slogan "Progress Not Perfection."

For some of us, having a sense of personal autonomy can be a challenge. Before recovery, we might have been so focused on what others thought of us that we only identified ourselves as part of a couple, part of a group, or part of a family and did not recognize our worth as individuals. Because of the effects upon us of another person's sex addiction, some of us have given little thought to our own value. As we grow in our understanding of program principles, we come to see that we do matter and have value — this is essential to our recovery. When we can recognize our autonomy, we can better appreciate the importance of good self-care. As we surrender our people-pleasing behavior to our Higher Power, we begin to recognize our inherent worth and growing ability to act on our own behalf.

For others of us, the challenge may lie in recognizing that other people matter just as much as we do. Perhaps we are used to insisting that things always go our way and be done to our liking. Suffering from the effects of sex addiction on our lives, many of us have experienced the desire to control.

There are also those of us who struggle with both aspects; sometimes we undervalue ourselves, and at other times we overinflate our own importance.

Tradition Four broadens our perspective and helps us to see the importance of both exercising our autonomy and showing consideration for our common welfare in all of our relationships. Practicing Tradition Four can create more serenity in our lives as we learn to better value and respect ourselves and others.

•   •   •

TRADITION FOUR QUESTIONS

*Each group should be autonomous,
except in matters affecting another group
or S-Anon or SA as a whole.*

1. How does my group express its autonomy? How does my group consider the impact of its decisions on other groups and on S-Anon as a whole?

2. How does my group take responsibility for its actions? Do we try to control other groups?

3. When my group makes a decision, do we consider the long-term, far-reaching consequences? If a decision does not work out, are we willing to take a group conscience to make the necessary changes?

4. How do I show my support for the spiritual principles of this program? Do I insist that I have a better way? If so, what has been the result?

5. How do I understand that the Traditions are guidelines and not laws? What does the idea of being obedient to the unenforceable mean to me? Do I trust the experience and wisdom of those who came before me and established the Traditions?

6. Do I try to make "rules" in my meetings, either overtly or covertly? Am I willing for the group members to decide the best way to handle situations?

7. Do I seek my Higher Power's guidance when making a decision about something in my meeting or home life? Am I aware when I am being self-serving or selfish versus when I am exercising self-care?

8. Am I flexible enough to allow other people and groups to be autonomous? Do I make an effort to familiarize myself with their point of view and pursue open lines of communication?

9. How do I handle situations where others do not follow my plans? Do I allow people room to make their own decisions and possible mistakes?

10. How do I take responsibility for myself? Do I accept and learn from the consequences of my own actions?

11. How do I practice autonomy in my daily life? When I am making a decision, do I consider how it will affect others? How do I find a balance?

TRADITION FIVE

❧

*Each S-Anon family group has but one purpose:
to help families of sexaholics. We do this by
practicing the Twelve Steps of S-Anon,
by encouraging and understanding our
sexaholic relatives, and by welcoming and
giving comfort to the families of sexaholics.*

Tradition Five offers us three valuable guides for how to pursue our primary purpose of helping those who have been negatively affected by the sexual behavior of another person. These suggestions have a broad impact on our lives and our fellowship. They help us to form healthy relationships with other people and ourselves. They ensure that the program will continue to be here to offer the same help to future S-Anon members, as well.

First, Tradition Five suggests that we actively practice the Twelve Steps of S-Anon. We may have come to S-Anon to find out how to "fix" the sex addict. However, eventually we recognize that we need help ourselves. It may take time to see how another person's sexual addiction has affected us. In trying to cope with sexaholism, whether or not we knew about it, we created unmanageability and emotional chaos. We find that until we thoughtfully examine our own attitudes and actions through working the Twelve Steps, it is unlikely that we can encourage, understand, or comfort anyone, including ourselves. By following the gentle guidance of the Twelve Steps, we come to trust in and rely on a Higher Power of our own understanding. We begin to take our eyes off the addict and focus on ourselves and our recovery. Our lives change as we learn to treat ourselves and others with acceptance, kindness, and love. Healthy, orderly thinking about our past, present, and future gradually replaces the distorted thinking that comes from being affected by this disease.

Second, learning about the nature of sex addiction and how it affects the entire family can give us a new perspective that helps us better understand our sexually-addicted relatives and friends. Even though their compulsive behavior hurts us deeply, we can acknowledge that the addicts also suffer. We begin to accept that this is a disease and that sex addicts are sick people. Understanding that addicts are powerless over their addiction to lust is one of the keys to our recovery. We can stop blaming the sexaholic, work through our genuine hurt and pain, and let go of the anger, bitterness, and resentment that have kept us locked in misery. We then become able to offer compassion and understanding based on what we can provide rather than on what the addict or others want or expect from us. Our self-respect grows as our changed attitudes allow us to treat the addict, as well as ourselves and all human beings, with compassion and respect. Only then can we begin to sow the first seeds of forgiveness.

"Encouraging" the sexaholic may at first sound like what we tried to do without success before we came to S-Anon. Through working the Twelve Steps, we may see that what we previously labeled "encouraging" behavior was actually quite controlling or enabling. Our intent was to get the addict to stop acting out. Once we realize our powerlessness over any other human being, we can look at what it means to "encourage" in a healthy way. With trust in our Higher Power, we find courage to detach with love and learn to set healthy boundaries for ourselves. Staying on our side of the street helps both the addict and us. As we keep the focus on ourselves and work our own program, we can begin to let go of shame, blame, and the desire to punish or to wallow in self-pity. When the situation warrants, we may recognize and affirm the sexaholic's progress without comparing or enabling. In any case, when we feel led to do so, we can always pray for him or her.

Over time, we become better able to let go of our need to control outcomes and other people. We begin to accept that people have the freedom to make their own choices, even if we disagree. We discern and follow our Higher Power's will for our relationships, even though it may be different from our own will. In some situations, we may decide to continue a relationship, and in other circumstances, we may need to let it go. There may be times when safety is a concern, and taking steps to care for our children and ourselves is crucial.

Our lives improve when we start to practice good self-care. God helps us to shed our guilt, shame, and hostility as we come to understand that this disease is not a personal reflection on us. When we surrender our self-righteous attitudes, we see more clearly that the disease of sex addiction is one part of a person, not the whole person.

Third, there are various ways that we can foster a welcoming and compassionate spirit at our S-Anon meetings. A warm smile goes a long way to ease the discomfort that newcomers may feel. We stay after meetings to talk with them and to introduce our S-Anon literature. Newcomers can be greatly encouraged when we openly share our own recovery and offer them the help and comfort that we have been privileged to receive. We share what our experience has been and what has helped us, which can provide hope to those who are still suffering. We urge newcomers to look for the similarities in our stories, rather than the differences, and to keep what they can relate to and leave the rest. Telling our S-Anon story and hearing the stories of others is an important part of our recovery journey and a vital service to our groups.

We offer up-to-date contact information so that newcomers may call or email other members, and we ask if they would appreciate a call, as well. We encourage them to attend at least six meetings before deciding if S-Anon is for them. Most meetings close with, "Keep coming back!" We keep in mind that all members, not only newcomers, need welcome and comfort. No matter how long we have been attending, we all benefit from the understanding and compassionate spirit at our meetings. These are just a few ways that we can be of service, which is so essential in keeping our fellowship healthy and able to help families and friends of sexaholics.

Working Tradition Five benefits all aspects of our lives. Discovering the advantages of clarifying and maintaining our primary purpose in all our endeavors helps us in our homes, our jobs, and our communities. When we clearly identify any goal, it becomes easier to see which activities are important and which are not only unnecessary but also might undermine our ability to achieve that goal. We experience less stress and gain a greater sense of satisfaction when we ask our Higher Power to show us what we need to do and how to accomplish it.

Focusing on and applying the principles of S-Anon to our own lives will, over time, bring about the promised gifts of the program. As we learn to live more fully in recovery, overcoming the effects of sexaholism one day at a time, we demonstrate to ourselves and others that change is possible, that the program works, and that it works when we work it. This, in itself, offers hope to all who come to S-Anon.

•   •   •

It is so easy for me to get off track and stumble in my recovery. Recently I started obsessing about my partner's health problem and rehearsing in my mind the "suggestions" that I thought would fix everything. When I told him what I would do in such a situation, I might have ended up coming across as judgmental. I think I insinuated that he was incapable of handling his own life. He became silent and withdrew. I realized I had not used the wise guidance of Tradition Five to first practice the Twelve Steps for myself. If I had done so, I might have discovered how much my fear can throw me off balance.

With this insight, I now feel more confident and humbled to share with a newcomer who may have experienced a similar situation, "I think I know something about what you are going through." When I serve my group by sharing my stumbles and successes along my recovery journey, my compassion, patience, and understanding have a chance to grow.

• • •

Through S-Anon, I am learning a new way of encouraging the sexaholic in my life. I used to think that the best way was to explain to her what I thought she was doing wrong and what she should do instead. I made it very clear to her which recovery program I thought she should work and which therapist she should see. Before S-Anon, I never caught on to the fact that this approach did not work; I only thought it had not worked yet, but I was convinced that it could and would.

My Higher Power is helping me to let go of monitoring her recovery. I realize that she has her own path and does not benefit from my criticism and interference. I no longer tell her to call her sponsor or to work the Steps. I try not to compare my progress in recovery to hers. She has her own Higher Power, and that is not my job description.

I want to recognize the positive things she does. I appreciate her work in recovery and offer silent support by being grateful rather than complaining about the time it takes. I try to stay in reality about her disease and keep my focus on myself. I am so grateful to S-Anon for showing me a healthier and more peaceful way of life.

• • •

Tradition Five talks about "encouraging and understanding our sexaholic relatives." I grew up with the disease of sex addiction in my home. My mother and my brother are the sex addicts that affected my life first, long before I married a sex addict. I often felt ashamed of my mother and embarrassed by her behavior. My brother was already a young adult when I was born, and I was abused by him. I always hated him and had very little contact with him as an adult. If we ran into each other, I would not speak to him, and I would often walk out of the room.

Through my recovery work in S-Anon, I was able to develop compassion and understanding. By working the Steps, I was able to look at my anger and resentments and move toward forgiveness. Then I was able to actually practice Tradition Five in my daily life with my mother. She died two years ago, and today I am very grateful that I was able to be her caregiver for the last few years of her life. I treated her with love, kindness, and compassion. I also forgave my brother, and I no longer hate him. He still is not a safe person for me, so I choose not to have a relationship with him, but I can pray for him. I try to keep in mind that my brother is also a family member of a sexaholic, so he deserves compassion. I am able to greet him with kindness if I occasionally have contact with him, and that feels like a miracle.

• • •

I was full of fear and anxiety about many things when I came to my first meeting. I had discovered my husband's sexaholism and realized my marriage was in serious trouble. As some people shared about their situations, I noticed that they were actually smiling and speaking about some of their problems in the past tense. This was my first hint that maybe there was a solution to this mess. I felt a glimmer of hope. If the leader had not invited me to share,

I probably would not have. When I spoke, it sounded like I was telling someone else's story; I still couldn't believe that these things were really happening to me.

As part of welcoming newcomers to our meeting, some members share a little about what brought them to S-Anon. The purpose of this is to help newcomers feel like they belong. However, after listening to those shares, I wondered if I could find help here because my story seemed much worse. After the meeting, one woman came up to me and told me her story, which was almost identical to mine. We talked for almost an hour, and she gave me her phone number. I realize today (eleven years later) that if that woman had not approached me, I might not be sitting here today enjoying the wonders of recovery: "serenity, dignity, and emotional growth."

Tradition Five teaches me that I can welcome and give comfort to others affected by sex addiction through service, and that service to our groups can be as simple and powerful as telling our story to others. I am very grateful.

•   •   •

When I first came to S-Anon, I had no understanding of the term "primary purpose" and how I could apply that in many situations to make my life more serene. After my spouse and I both started attending recovery meetings, I had visions of our relationship suddenly becoming what I had always hoped it would be. If we went on a trip, for example, I thought it would be a wonderful opportunity to "get away together" and "grow closer." I would become so disappointed when this did not magically happen. My sponsor patiently suggested to me that I might consider the primary purpose of the trip and focus on that. For example, when we took a trip to see our son who lived out of town, she pointed out that the primary purpose was to visit with our son. When we went to the art museum, she reminded me that the primary purpose was to see the museum's exhibits.

I discovered that when I was able to focus on the primary purpose of whatever the trip or activity was, I was able to appreciate it and feel satisfied. When I unrealistically expected the activity to

expand beyond its primary purpose to include mending our fractured relationship, I was disappointed. My sponsor's insights on
the benefits of clarifying and staying focused on the primary purpose have helped me to stay in reality and to enjoy the many good
things in my life.

•   •   •

PRACTICING
THESE
PRINCIPLES

❦

L iving with or having lived with sex addiction can impact us
deeply, but when we start going to S-Anon meetings, we begin
to feel better and believe there
is hope. However, feeling a little relief can tempt us to only
attend meetings without actually working the Steps. If we
do this, we will cheat ourselves
and miss out on the promised
gifts of the program. The Steps
might seem overwhelming or
confusing at first, but they are
the gateway to a new way of
life. Working the Twelve Steps

*I found an S-Anon
group, and in that
group, I found the help,
unconditional love, and
support I desperately
needed.[7]*

is usually neither easy nor fast, nor do we work through them
perfectly or just once. The benefits are many, including gaining a
greater sense of reality and of our strengths and shortcomings. We
develop a new confidence as we let go of our shame and accept ourselves as we are, perhaps for the very first time. As we learn to place
our trust in a Power greater than ourselves, our anxiety lessens and
we experience a new peace. We begin to feel hope as we see that
there is a solution. Eventually,we are inspired to carry the message
to others who are still suffering.

The second suggestion in Tradition Five, that we encourage
and understand our sexaholic relatives, might at first cause some
of us to balk. Have we not tried to encourage and understand the
addict even though we ourselves were feeling so much pain? Are
we perhaps still seeing ourselves as victims? Over time it becomes

---

[7] *Reflections of Hope,* p. 4.

apparent that dwelling on this feeling of resentment does not help our recovery. Accepting that sex addiction is a disease with specific symptoms is difficult, but it is an important hurdle that we can overcome with time in recovery. Releasing our own resentment and bitterness frees us from feeling and acting like victims and allows us to consider the possibility of extending compassion to the addict.

Tradition Five is also about developing compassion for ourselves. We learn, heal, and grow by working the S-Anon program. At times we may still feel triggered by the sexaholic's behavior, but our own recovery becomes our focus. This helps us to detach with love and find serenity, whether the addict is still acting out or not. Gaining a broader understanding of addiction, obsession, and compulsion encourages us to forgive others as well as ourselves.

Our compassion for the sexaholic grows when we begin to see her or him as a fellow struggler rather than as an enemy. We learn to treat the sex addict as we would like to be treated. Encouraging our sexaholic relatives and friends can consist of encouraging them to find their own path and allowing them the dignity of doing so without judgment, criticism, or interference. It does not consist of our telling them what they are doing wrong, doing things for them such as paying bills or maintaining their vehicle, insisting they work a specific program or seek therapy or medical help, or saying that they can go right ahead and continue to ruin their own lives. Encouragement means that we recognize and appreciate the positive things they do, but we do not condone and no longer participate in activities that are unhealthy for us. If they decide to engage in risky behaviors, we can respectfully say that we do not feel safe. We neither shame nor blame them for their decisions.

The third suggestion of Tradition Five, to welcome and give comfort to the families of sexaholics, is a balm for many of us, no matter our relationship with sexually addicted people. Before we came into the program, we may have thought that we would never find comfort and understanding. Whatever feelings we may have when we begin our recovery in S-Anon are common and completely understandable. We may think our stories and feelings are unique, but since the effects of sexaholism upon us are the same, we can gain strength by joining together to seek recovery. Many of us discovered that our first experience of unconditional love and acceptance occurred in the S-Anon fellowship

We show compassion to all who find their way to S-Anon. We become more open to loving others who are on a similar, challenging journey. However, we do not take on another's burdens that do not belong to us. We do not give advice, and we cannot solve other people's problems. We respect the right of others to make their own choices. We can work together, gaining strength from our Higher Power, the S-Anon program, our sponsor, and other members. We discover that we have the power to set our own limits on what we will and will not do in all our relationships and in all areas of our lives.

Tradition Five offers hope for all family members and friends of sex addicts. Some of us come into these rooms afraid for our children, and we are sometimes ashamed of what they may have experienced growing up in our homes. However, as we change through working the program, they will begin to see the gifts of S-Anon in action. We now have tools to share with them that help us to find serenity no matter our outward circumstances. One of these available tools is S-Ateen, a Twelve Step program designed specifically for our teenage family members just as S-Anon is for our adult family members.

With its focus on our primary purpose, Tradition Five also helps us see the broader picture in our daily lives. For example, for those of us with children, one primary purpose might be to love and nurture them. As we work the Steps, we come to see that our obsession with the sex addict in our lives interferes with our ability to give our children the care and consideration they need. As we surrender our obsession and ask our Higher Power to remove it, we become better able to focus on what we can do to achieve our goal of loving and nurturing our children.

We can sometimes feel overwhelmed by the effects upon us of another person's sexual addiction, but when we focus on our primary purpose and ask our Higher Power for direction to do the next right thing, we can feel more peace and serenity. We can trust the process as we experience progress and growth, sometimes quickly, sometimes slowly, one day at a time.

•   •   •

TRADITION FIVE QUESTIONS

Each S-Anon Family Group has but one purpose: to help families of sexaholics. We do this by practicing the Twelve Steps of S-Anon, by encouraging and understanding our sexaholic relatives, and by welcoming and giving comfort to the families of sexaholics.

1. How do I work the Twelve Steps in a thorough and thoughtful way? How does my Higher Power guide me in this? Have I been able to accept the guidance and help of a sponsor to work the Twelve Steps?

2. How do the members of my group help each other practice the Twelve Steps of S-Anon? In what ways do we use our Conference Approved Literature?

3. Do I understand that sexaholism is a disease? How has working the S-Anon Twelve Steps helped me find compassion for the sexaholic? What else has helped? What does encouraging and understanding the sexaholic mean to me?

4 What does my group do to inform the community about S-Anon? Are people able to learn about S-Anon and locate our meetings?

5. How do I welcome and give comfort to the newcomer? What did I find welcoming and encouraging when I first came to S-Anon?

6. How do I describe the primary purpose of S-Anon to newcomers? How do I give away what I have received in the program?

7. Am I mindful that long-term members can also still suffer? How do I reach out and encourage those who have been in the program a long time or who return after a lengthy absence?

8. Do I believe I have something to offer others, and do I listen and learn from them as well? How do I interact with members I may find difficult?

9. How does my recovery help my children? Are there any tools of the program that I would like to share with them? Are there teenagers in my life who might benefit from S-Ateen?

10. In what ways am I able to clarify my primary purposes in my daily life?

TRADITION SIX

❧

*Our S-Anon Family Groups ought never endorse,
finance, or lend our name to any outside enterprise,
lest problems of money, property, and prestige divert
us from our primary spiritual aim.
Although a separate entity, we should always
cooperate with Sexaholics Anonymous.*

Tradition Six encourages us to keep our attention on our primary purpose as a group: to help families and friends of sexaholics. We undermine our objectives and our ability to help others and ourselves if we lose sight of our spiritual aim of recovery. In order to keep our meetings healthy and productive, we devote them solely to S-Anon. This prevents us from being distracted and straying from the S-Anon principles, which would interfere with our personal recovery and Twelfth Step work.

We learn the importance of focus. Tradition Six reminds us that if we do not keep our attention exclusively on our spiritual goals, we can easily slide into areas that could harm our fellowship and sabotage our own recovery. Involvement with outside enterprises may entangle us with issues of money and property. We can have problems of prestige as well. Prestige involves the perception of our status and reputation among others. Many of us experience low self-esteem as a result of "living with or having lived with" a sexaholic. This can lead to an excessive desire for praise and admiration. With the help of our Higher Power and our S-Anon recovery, we begin to gain a sense of self-worth that is not dependent upon the opinions of others.

For these reasons, we do not endorse, fund, finance, recommend, or lend our name to any outside enterprise. By outside enterprises, we mean any venture that is not directly a part of S-Anon, such as businesses, political organizations, religions, recovery programs, other Twelve Step groups, therapists, treatment programs, charities, research projects, social media, films, or outside literature. We do not make announcements about events for other Twelve Step programs, even if their principles are similar to ours. Some S-Anon members may attend other Twelve Step meetings, but they do not mention them during our meetings. We keep the focus on the S-Anon solution and point of view.

As individuals, we are free to pursue any avenues to recovery and make any personal choices that we wish. However, we avoid doing so as representatives of S-Anon or during S-Anon meetings. Recommending or discussing a therapist or treatment facility during our meetings could create confusion, division, or an impression that another activity was necessary for recovery. Our members, especially newcomers, could get the impression that we are a health service, educational or therapy program, or research project. We do not want to imply that our primary purpose is anything other than helping families and friends of sex addicts recover from the effects upon us of another person's sex addiction.

S-Anon is a spiritual program, but it is not affiliated with any religion. We assure newcomers that the use of the word "God" in our meetings is not an endorsement of any particular religion or spiritual belief. "The God of our understanding" implies a power greater than ourselves — our own Higher Power. We speak of the value that prayer and meditation have in our recovery, but we do not prescribe specific religious practices. Whether or not we are affiliated with any particular religion, we are all welcome in S-Anon. We focus only on our shared spiritual goals.

It is important that S-Anon groups remain unencumbered. That is, we do not own property except for basic materials necessary to conduct our meetings. We pay rent or give a regular donation to indicate there is no affiliation with the meeting venue, and we do not use the name of the meeting location as part the name of the group.

We donate our Seventh Tradition money to support only S-Anon activities, such as our World Service Office, Intergroup, community outreach, or local recovery events. Giving S-Anon funds to an outside enterprise, even if it seems related to our spiritual aim, might be seen as an endorsement of that enterprise and a dilution of the program. Offering group money to support members with their personal needs is another example of an outside issue that would undermine our primary purpose. However, groups or Intergroups can offer event scholarships if they wish.

We cooperate with Sexaholics Anonymous, and we may extend this cooperation to other sexual addiction fellowships, as well. We do this by working together for a common goal, such as planning recovery events. However, we remain independent and do not endorse, affiliate with, or align ourselves with any other fellowship.

As we explore the wisdom of Tradition Six in our group, we become more aware of how to apply it both to ourselves and to our interactions with others. We remember the importance of our serenity, integrity, and spirituality. We may find, as individuals, that our commitment to recovery can easily become diverted. We stay mindful of how problems of money, property, and prestige can also impact our personal lives. We consider limiting or avoiding activities and relationships that could be harmful. Eventually, we become more aware of how we spend our time and learn to keep "first things first" to minimize the effects of those distractions.

The benefits of working the S-Anon program become evident in the way we treat other people. We can cooperate and connect with others without losing part of ourselves. We avoid being overly supportive emotionally, physically, financially, and spiritually. After examining our motives, we may find that we do not need to advise or control others or get our own way in order to prove our self-worth. We mind our own business and not anyone else's. Rather than imposing our own agendas or prescriptions for "right" living on others, we respect their freedom to discover directions and solutions for themselves. We live and let live.

•　　•　　•

Tradition Six
STORIES

I get a deeper understanding of this Tradition by applying it to my personal life, rather than just to my group. For instance, sometimes I allow financial concerns to take too much priority over my spiritual life. The other day as I was meditating, I started to think about something I thought I needed to buy. I now realize why I was distracted. I have a fear of overextending myself financially, which would require me to work a lot longer before I could retire. I got so afraid about this situation that I spent time worrying about it at the expense of my serenity.

I also sometimes struggle with wanting to appear like I always have it all together, which diverts me from my own spiritual aim. As part of this, I pride myself on keeping my personal issues out of my work life. However, one week I was feeling very tired and worn down. A colleague pointed out that I appeared to be having a bad day. I realized I was feeling overextended, resentful, and frustrated. I felt embarrassed and sad that my lack of serenity was apparent enough for someone to notice. I have spent a lot of time worrying about what others think of me. With the help of my group and my Higher Power, I am learning not to base my worth on the opinions of other people.

With the guidance of Tradition Six, I can learn to put aside problems of money, property, and prestige in order to let my primary spiritual aim lead me through life.

• • •

At the time I found out that my spouse was an active sexaholic, I was a new mom, jobless, and nearly devoid of my own identity. My only definition of myself revolved around my family. Having a spouse who was acting out led me to think I wasn't good enough. If I was enough, how could he look elsewhere? I simply crumbled. Depression is an understatement. Those were dark days.

In time, I found S-Anon. Going to meetings was the first individual action I had taken in a long time. I had entirely lost myself in the roles of mother, daughter, and wife. I had lost myself in trying to get my husband sober. Really, I had lost myself in many ways. S-Anon helped me reclaim *me*.

While Tradition Six talks about many other things, it was the first place that I saw the idea of being a "separate entity" — and these two words are invaluable to me. I had been giving others power over me because I didn't realize I was distinct and important on my own. I was a stranger to myself. I felt really sad about that. I began asking my Higher Power to enable my voice. I prayed to get to know myself again, and for the splintered pieces of my womanhood to be reunited into the person God intended me to be.

As I did the work that the Steps, Traditions, and Concepts of Service laid out for me, God helped me to discover and accept myself — my story, my assets, my defects, my sexuality, my parenting, my artistic self, and my sense of humor. These things had been lost to me for so long. As I grew in my autonomy, I could detach more easily and was able to let my spouse be his own person, too. I came to accept both of us as individuals.

Today, I know that I am a separate being. I can choose to cooperate as situations occur, or I can choose to walk away. I can ask myself what I believe, what I feel is right, and what it is that I want to do. I can pray and meditate. I can seek mentorship from others in program who share their decisions and experiences. I can take my time and decide how to participate. I don't have to lose myself in someone else's ideas or disease. I am separate. I am enough. I am.

• • •

The father of an S-Anon member called our S-Anon Helpline and requested a meeting with someone to answer his questions about our program and how it worked. I volunteered to meet with him at a coffee shop.

This gentleman was in a lot of pain over how sexaholism had impacted his daughter's marriage. I described the Twelve Steps of S-Anon and how we, as members, do not offer advice or have an opinion about whether someone should stay in a marriage or leave it, but we do offer a solution to the problem of obsessing about another person's behavior. I suggested that attending meetings might be helpful because we can meet others who have been through similar situations and learn how they found serenity. I invited him to attend a meeting because, as a family member, he also was affected by the disease of sexaholism.

As I shared, I sensed that he seemed to get some relief by talking about the problem. At the end of our conversation, he asked me what he could pay for my time. I explained that I was not a therapist or counselor, just a grateful recovering member of S-Anon. I said that I could not accept payment, as that would be breaking our Traditions.

Afterwards, I realized that I am not immune to problems of property and prestige. I felt extremely proud that he thought that I deserved to be paid for our conversation. However, I went way beyond feeling glad I could be of service. I began to think of my contribution to the conversation as my wisdom rather than as the wisdom of S-Anon. I also thought about his offer of money. Even though I knew I could not accept any payment, my thoughts still raced to how helpful that would have been with my tight budget.

I thought and prayed about this whole encounter and was reminded of something crucial. The S-Anon program is a spiritual one. With the help of my Higher Power and the guidance of the program, I can detect when I am heading off course. I can then examine my motives and make a course correction back to my spiritual path.

•   •   •

When I first started attending S-Anon meetings, I was so eager to learn about sexaholism and to get help. One evening I could not wait to tell my fellow members about the latest book my counselor had suggested I read and about a conference she thought I should attend. I hoped that they would read the book and go to the conference with me.

Another time during a meeting, I quoted my counselor. I felt like her recommendation would carry added weight and prestige. For example, rather than just telling how I had confronted my partner, I said my counselor had advised me to make a list — I had a long one — of all his transgressions and confront him with those, one at a time. I didn't realize how it could have been very easy for the inexperienced S-Anon listener to adhere to this "professional" advice and attempt the same, which could have had dire consequences.

Fortunately, in both instances a more experienced S-Anon member gently urged me to discuss only S-Anon resources during our meeting. At the time, I didn't really understand the implications of her words. They seemed narrow-minded to me. As time went on and I learned more about the Traditions, I began to see how important it is not to muddy the waters, but rather to stay focused on these S-Anon principles.

• • •

It took me some time to appreciate the wisdom of this Tradition. Early in my S-Anon recovery, I had a sponsor whose son had a medical condition. The local association for this condition was sponsoring a fundraiser that she was helping to plan. I offered to help with the event, and I suggested that she announce this at a meeting to solicit help from the other members of our S-Anon group. In my mind, this seemed like a natural thing to do, and I felt that many members would be happy to help. Fortunately, my sponsor was a firm believer in the Traditions, and she patiently explained to me that this would be violating Tradition Six. At the time, I did not understand, and I thought that she was passing up a great opportunity.

Later I was able to look back on this and see how misguided I was. I needed some relief from the pain that brought me to S-Anon before I could even begin to understand the Traditions. I found that relief through the S-Anon program. Taking time during our meetings for these kinds of announcements would have been taking time away from the message of recovery. My focus during the meetings might have switched to the personal announcements rather than on recovering from the effects upon me of living with the disease of sexaholism. I came to S-Anon for help. Tradition Six ensures that S-Anon meetings stay one hundred percent focused on offering that help to all of our members.

• • •

PRACTICING
THESE
PRINCIPLES

ॐ

It can take some time to learn and embrace the many new and different approaches to life that S-Anon offers. As newcomers, we often do not realize the difference between healthy and unhealthy behavior. We might initially view our meetings as the perfect opportunity to promote fundraising activities or business endeavors. After meeting with others on a weekly basis for some time, we often develop trust and a sense of mutual support. However, we do not impose upon our members or take advantage of their trust. We keep our relationships on a spiritual level and do not complicate them by asking other members to buy jewelry, cookies, school raffle tickets or any other products or services at S-Anon meetings.

If we mentioned names of therapists, treatment centers, or self-help books in our meetings or advertised them in S-Anon publications, we would seem to be endorsing them and associating the S-Anon name with them, potentially distracting us from our primary spiritual aim.[8]

We do not ask others to help us or other organizations by participating in any fundraising activities. We avoid any kind of pressure by never asking anyone to buy anything. We stay dedicated to our primary purpose and do not allow outside activities to complicate, disrupt, or dilute our spiritual message and goals.

---

[8] *Working the S-Anon Program,* p. 33.

Along with these guidelines, we do not promote anything that is not S-Anon, such as literature that is not Conference Approved, announcements, order forms, therapy referrals, or therapeutic models, because promotion is a form of endorsement. This may feel difficult at first. We have no way of knowing if any of these things might indeed prove beneficial to any other individual. We remind ourselves that we are each on our own spiritual path and cannot presume or judge what will be best for others.

Tradition Six gives us an opportunity to look at ourselves to see if a desire for prestige might be part of our motives. What might keep us from following the guidance of S-Anon to stay focused on its message? Perhaps we have low self-esteem, or on the other hand, we might think we have superior knowledge and insight. Why are we not content just to be a member among members? If we think we are guided solely by a desire to help, do we truly understand that keeping the S-Anon program strong, clear, and unencumbered is one of the best ways we can help ourselves and our fellow members?

If we are members of a particular faith community, we take special care not to promote our religion. Our particular faith may have a name or terms for a Higher Power that we have always used, but we refrain from using these during meetings out of respect for the spiritually inclusive nature of our program. We use "my Higher Power" or "the God of my understanding" instead. We also are careful not to quote any religious material or use any prayers from a specific religion during our meetings.

Either as a group or as individual members, we may reach out with S-Anon Conference Approved Literature or Service Literature to others, such as therapists, physicians, lawyers, nearby colleges, or local jails. We do not consider this outreach endeavor an affiliation, but rather Twelfth Step work. We stay distinct and separate, but we may offer information about the S-Anon path to recovery for those who qualify for our program.

Cooperation is important in our families and personal lives, but we closely examine how, when, and where to do that. We cooperate with others only as far as we are able to do so without becoming enmeshed in their lives and trying to control them. We maintain our loving detachment and individuality. By asking our Higher Power for guidance and our sponsor for input, we learn to set boundaries for healthy cooperation with others.

Our primary spiritual aim is to live healthy and peaceful lives, knowing that our Higher Power is in control and guiding our path in recovery. If we get sidetracked, taking a thorough personal inventory of distracting issues can help steer us back to our spiritual path. We remember to "keep it simple" and examine issues that might be overcomplicating our lives, such as being too busy, getting too carried away with projects, or becoming overly involved in disputes. We keep our focus on our primary spiritual aim — our recovery.

• • •

TRADITION SIX QUESTIONS

Our S-Anon Family Groups ought never endorse, finance, or lend our name to any outside enterprise, lest problems of money, property, and prestige divert us from our primary spiritual aim. Although a separate entity, we should always cooperate with Sexaholics Anonymous.

1. What does primary spiritual aim mean to me? To my group? How might endorsing, financing, or lending the S-Anon name to outside enterprises be confusing or distract my meeting from its primary spiritual aim?

2. If I have received help from professional therapists, treatment centers, or self-help books, am I willing to refrain from mentioning them during meeting time? Do I understand that others might assume that S-Anon endorses them and associates with them?

3. Have I ever brought up outside issues or promoted my business or someone else's? Has anyone at a meeting or any other S-Anon event ever tried to sell any products, literature, philosophy, or religion? How could the Traditions guide us to respond in a healthy way?

4. How do I share with others that S-Anon is a spiritual program, not a religious program, and that all are welcome? How does my group stay focused on the S-Anon principles of recovery?

5. Do I use general terms such as God and Higher Power when sharing about my spiritual experiences and refrain from mentioning specific religious denominations, personalities, books, and prayers? Why does Tradition Six guide us to do this?

6. Is my S-Anon group named after the location where we meet, such as the church name or business building? How might this be confusing to a newcomer?

7. Do we use group funds only to support S-Anon? What is our idea of a prudent reserve?

8. Do I understand that all other Twelve Step programs are completely separate from S-Anon? Why are their events not announced at our meetings?

9. In what ways might money, property, or prestige divert me from my primary spiritual aim in other areas of my life?

10. How do I define cooperation? How can I cooperate with others in a healthy way without losing myself? How do I cooperate with fellowships for sex addicts without being diverted from my primary spiritual aim or my own responsibilities?

TRADITION SEVEN

❦

Every group ought to be fully self-supporting,
declining outside contributions.

The spiritual principle of accepting responsibility is inherent in Tradition Seven. It guides us to appreciate our resources and manage them. We maintain our freedom and autonomy when we are self-supporting by accepting responsibility for all aspects of our lives, not only financial, but emotional, spiritual, and physical as well. We learn not to expect others to do for us what we are capable of doing for ourselves, for our groups, and for our S-Anon worldwide fellowship.

With God's guidance many members, past and present, have worked together to ensure that S-Anon will be available for those who want its help. As S-Anon members, we share in the responsibility for our groups and the S-Anon fellowship as a whole. Our needs are basic, and it is up to us, and no one else, to see that we meet those needs. We ask our Higher Power to guide us in this process.

One of our needs is financial. In the spirit of Tradition Seven, we contribute funds to keep S-Anon running in order to help families and friends of sexaholics. S-Anon is not a club or society that charges dues or membership fees; we are a fellowship of equals with specific financial obligations. At our meetings, we usually pass a basket or envelope to collect donations to cover expenses such as rent, literature, and contributions to our worldwide fellowship. Each group may have a suggested amount for members to contribute, but it is never a requirement. We keep in mind the needs of our group and the S-Anon fellowship as we individually decide how much to contribute. Each group avoids retaining excess funds but determines and maintains a prudent reserve sufficient to cover short-term expenses.

S-Anon has financial needs beyond our local groups. Some areas have Intergroups that help S-Anon communities in various ways. They may maintain a telephone contact line, coordinate outreach, and plan local and regional recovery events. Beyond the local area, our World Service Office (WSO) is the central headquarters for S-Anon. It relies on financial contributions from groups and individual members and on the sale of S-Anon literature to run the office. This includes printing literature, serving as a point of contact for newcomers, and maintaining communication with our worldwide fellowship and the professional community. Just as we all have personal monthly expenses and bills to pay, the WSO has monthly expenses including rent, utilities, insurance, and salaries for paid staff. Therefore, it is important that each registered group send a monthly or quarterly financial contribution to the WSO.

S-Anon neither solicits nor accepts financial contributions from outside organizations, corporations, or individuals. No outside benefactor, no matter how well-intentioned, may donate funds or other support (such as free rent or printing) that could influence or even appear to influence how we run our meetings or S-Anon as a whole. Only S-Anon members may contribute money, voice opinions, and vote on matters pertaining to our fellowship. In addition, we do not accept a large monetary contribution from any individual member, since that could lead to a perception that he or she is entitled to more influence than other members. This financial limit, which is stated in the "Bylaws of the S-Anon International Family Groups, Inc. Board of Trustees," reinforces the principle that we are a fellowship of equals.

There are many other ways we can contribute to our group in addition to giving money. We attend meetings regularly; share our experience, strength, and hope; listen to others; and commit to service. As soon as we feel able, we may volunteer to set up chairs, display literature, clean up, or facilitate the meeting. We may get a sponsor and eventually sponsor someone else. We can take a turn serving in whichever positions our group might have, such as secretary, treasurer, or literature chairperson. As newcomers, we may need time just to listen, learn, and take care of ourselves. Through doing service, we learn to use our skills and develop new ones. We take time to seek our Higher Power's guidance and talk with our sponsor when we consider a service position. The support of a service sponsor is often helpful as we navigate how to do service and balance it with self-care. We want our group to continue to exist for us as well as others in the future, so we each do what we can.

As our recovery progresses, we consider what we can do to support the fellowship beyond the immediate needs of our local group. We grow in our awareness of and appreciation for the many different service positions that are necessary to carry the message of S-Anon recovery to those still struggling with the effects of sexaholism. Many S-Anon service opportunities exist. We may serve as an Intergroup Representative, an Area Delegate to the annual World Service Conference, or a member of the Board of Trustees. If our area hosts a recovery event, such as a marathon or an international convention, we can help in numerous ways, from serving on the planning committee to volunteering for service roles at the event itself. S-Anon's Board of Trustees has various Standing Committees that work on specific areas, such as maintaining good stewardship of our funds or developing new literature that is from the S-Anon point of view. We can volunteer to become trained to serve as a certified group sponsor for S-Ateen meetings. Our S-Anon/S-Ateen Service Manual offers a good description of our service structure and clarifies the duties and responsibilities of each position.

There are also ways to support the fellowship through S-Anon literature. When we purchase our literature, we support the WSO. Writing our stories and submitting them for use in future S-Anon literature help carry the message of our experience, strength, and hope. Only S-Anon members can understand and deliver the S-Anon message of hope because we have lived it. Countless members have volunteered to plan, write, read, and edit material in order to create and update the Conference Approved Literature and Service Literature we have today. We become more self-supporting as a recovery community with each new publication.

As a spiritual fellowship, we do not want one or even several members to carry too much service responsibility because our sense of mutual responsibility and respect could be undermined. S-Anon is self-supporting because together, under the guidance of a Higher Power, we all are responsible to keep it running. We serve in positions for a designated period of time, and we step down when that term is over to allow others to experience the benefits of doing service. The rotation of service positions helps to maintain and support a fellowship of equals under the guidance of a Higher Power. We try to do our part as willing volunteers, but we do not take on so much that we feel overwhelmed and resentful, which could jeopardize our recovery. We also keep in mind that if we take on too much, others might feel excluded and perhaps resentful as well. We have found that when only one or two people in a group assume all responsibilities, that group is no longer healthy or self-supporting.

As with all of the Traditions, Tradition Seven applies to us personally as well as to our group and fellowship. With our Higher Power's guidance, we learn how to take better care of ourselves in all aspects of our lives. We take responsibility for our financial, spiritual, emotional, and physical health. If our contribution to our household is not monetary, we still can participate in the financial decision-making. We learn to establish healthy boundaries and take responsibility for our actions and reactions; we discover that blaming others for our problems does not help us grow. We gain clarity about what is our responsibility and what is not. Periodically we may want to reevaluate our financial decisions, including our education and/or employment options.

We learn we can choose to take care of ourselves physically by eating healthy foods, exercising regularly, and managing stress. We can support ourselves emotionally by connecting with others, attending meetings, talking with our sponsor, and acknowledging our feelings. We begin to understand that a part of our self-support comes from learning how to relate to others in healthy ways, which include listening, sharing, asking for help when needed, and being open to feedback. Instead of depending on the opinions of others for our self-esteem, we learn to rely on our Higher Power and begin to trust our own inner voice.

We can also be self-supporting spiritually by exploring our beliefs and spending time in activities that we find spiritually uplifting, such as prayer and meditation with the Higher Power of our understanding, journaling, taking a walk, enjoying the beauty of nature, feeling grateful, and simply being mindful of the present moment. When we put these suggestions and the tools of our program to work in our lives, we begin to experience "the wonders of serenity, dignity, and emotional growth." [9]

Through our study of Tradition Seven, we gain a fuller understanding of our responsibilities to ourselves, our Higher Power, and other people. We learn to embrace a healthy independence while accepting the need for a healthy interdependence with others. We ask our Higher Power to help us find balance between them in all areas of our lives.

• • •

---

[9] *Working the S-Anon Program,* p. 131.

M y reaction to my husband's addiction to pornography led me to S-Anon and helped me to appreciate Tradition Seven. My money was in a joint bank account with his, but I realized that I did not want to have my name or money

associated in any way with an account used to pay for pornography. With the guidance of my Higher Power, I decided it was time for me to put Tradition Seven into active use. I needed to become self-supporting financially.

Even as I was hoping for signs of my husband's recovery, I began to move toward separating our finances and managing my money according to my own principles. Sadly, he chose not to pursue recovery, and we are now in the process of ending our marriage. The good news is that because I took Tradition Seven into my life as a guideline, I am ready to lead my life as a financially self-supporting person. I am grateful that my Higher Power opened my eyes and gave me direction through this Tradition.

• • •

W hen I attended my first few S-Anon meetings, I would stop listening whenever the Traditions were read. They didn't seem to offer any insights or suggestions to help me keep the sex addict sexually sober, which was my goal at the time. The Traditions seemed more like "housekeeping rules" than anything else. I didn't understand why we couldn't just skip them and cut to the chase—announce the topic and begin sharing.

Because I lived with a spouse who was not dependable, the necessity of Tradition Seven made perfect sense to me. Of course my meeting ought to be "fully self-supporting." Of course we needed to collect enough money each week to pay our group expenses and contribute to our fellowship. We needed people there every week, sharing experience, strength, and hope. I did my best to get to my meeting, even when it wasn't convenient. I made sure I had cash with me each week so I could contribute, ever mindful of the pain I had felt when I first walked through the door of S-Anon. I am grateful that my contributions help to ensure that S-Anon will continue to be there for newcomers in the future.

Then I heard, "...declining outside contributions." I questioned why we wouldn't accept with gratitude any funds that might come our way. I believed that S-Anon was, most certainly, a *very* worthy cause. As an enthusiastic newcomer, I wanted to stand on a mountain and spread the news about our program to the world. In the past, I had worked with other non-profit organizations that had actively pursued donations from local businesses and individuals. Why didn't S-Anon?

Over time, I began to understand the reason. The only way S-Anon could keep its autonomy was by not becoming indebted to any person or entity and by not accepting financial or any other type of help from non-members. Thinking back on my previous experiences, I realized that most donors were willing to support a cause in exchange for advertising space or some other support for their business or organization. Now I understand better why S-Anon values Tradition Seven so much.

•   •   •

One way that I can be personally self-supporting is to stop my self-defeating behaviors. When I first came to S-Anon, I did not recognize that expecting my spouse to read my mind and take care of me was self-defeating. I thought I could read her mind, and my well-being was dependent on how she was doing. If she was happy, I was happy; if she was angry, I was angry.

Slowly I began to release my grip on my sexaholic spouse. I realized that I was enmeshed with her. Through working the program, I began to see myself as an individual, both separate and significant. I began to consider how I could meet my own needs. Now, I don't depend on others to make me happy. I can take responsibility, one day at a time, for meeting my needs--spiritually, emotionally, socially, and physically. I can be proactive in improving my conscious contact with God. I don't have to wait for someone to go with me to pursue my spiritual growth. I can do things for myself and by myself as well as with others. At times my spouse and I do things together, but my ability to enjoy myself now is not contingent upon my being part of a couple. I am grateful for my progress.

• • •

In addition to my S-Anon group, I belong to several other "groups." My husband and I are a "group." I have to pay attention to my part in spending our money, paying bills, saving for the future, and participating in household chores. When we discuss how to spend and save our money, I speak up for my wants and needs. I let go of control and try to consider his opinions, realizing that I don't have the final say in every financial decision.

My friends and I are also a "group." I have learned that one of the keys to a successful friendship is to pay my own way. Although it can be nice to treat a friend to lunch or listen to her problems, if I continually pick up the tab – financially or emotionally – I may be enabling someone else and not be taking good care of myself. I could begin to resent the other person. I feel so much better when I participate as a mutual partner in my friendships.

In my work "group," I have learned not to automatically rush in to save the day when another employee does not do his or her part of the work. We all need help at times, but it is very easy for me to fall into a pattern of rescuing and then resenting others when there is a crisis. Tradition Seven is helping me step back and allow others to become self-supporting, too.

• • •

While on summer vacation, I dropped in to see my cousin and his family. They welcomed me in and we chatted for a while. When I used their bathroom, I realized that nothing happened when I tried to turn on the light. I became aware of coolers in the bathtub. I returned to the living room and noted that the usual electronic equipment failed to display a time or even flashing numbers. The realization sunk in that they had no electricity. I so wanted to make things right as I defined right. I immediately felt responsible for rescuing their four children. However, I noted that there seemed to be plenty of food in the house, so the children were not going hungry. Even so, the sense of wanting to fix this was huge. I sat there with my discomfort and obsessively thought about what to do. I chose not to do anything.

After leaving, I replayed the situation in my mind. Tradition Seven kept reminding me, "Every group ought to be fully self-supporting, declining outside contributions." Other family members have repeatedly bailed my cousin out of one situation or another. Recovery taught me that he had not asked for my help and that offering him money would not solve his situation.

Several months later, my cousin called me. He had started a new job a few weeks after I was there, and things were going well. I thanked my Higher Power for guiding me to allow my cousin the dignity of finding his own path.

•   •   •

PRACTICING
THESE
PRINCIPLES

∝

As we grow in our appreciation of the balance and peace of mind that come from being self-supporting, we consider more carefully how to apply Tradition Seven to our group and to our lives outside of the group. We realize that S-Anon groups benefit from good care, just as we do. The Twelve Traditions offer groups helpful suggestions to establish and maintain group health. Problems will arise from time to time. When they do, we acknowledge them and work together to find a solution. Taking a group conscience can help. We take the time necessary to fully discuss and consider options and various solutions.

> *Tradition Seven...*
> *encourages me to take*
> *action on behalf of my*
> *own needs, without*
> *expecting someone else to*
> *come to my rescue.*[10]

An example of a group problem might concern service. We might have members who continually do all of the work and others who have not considered stepping into a service role. If we recognize that the same people remain in the service positions, we may call for a group conscience to discuss rotation of service. Having applied a spiritual solution to our personal recovery work, we recognize we can also apply a spiritual solution to any difficulties that we have as a group. We let go of outcomes and make room for our Higher Power to guide us.

We can apply Tradition Seven to our personal lives by reflecting on what it means to be self-supporting as individuals. As the

---

[10] *Reflections of Hope*, p. 366.

S-Anon Problem states, "We chose friends and partners who could not or would not love and support us in a healthy way." We may not have known what healthy support looked like. Many of us wanted someone to take care of us and to fill the void inside of us that only our Higher Power could fill. We thought that if we could just find someone to support us in the way we wanted, then we would be fine. We often had no concept of being self-supporting emotionally, spiritually, financially, physically, or in any other way. There is a spiritual solution. Becoming more self-supporting is a process. Learning what our true needs are and seeking options to meet them are both part of being self-supporting. With the Higher Power of our understanding to guide us, one day at a time, we find a satisfying solution to our hunger for love and support.

Living with the effects of sexual addiction may have distorted our idea of self-support. Some of us felt like victims and expected others to rescue and take care of us. Others felt we were the only responsible ones. We shouldered the responsibilities of others who appeared to us to be unwilling or unable to do things for themselves. Some of us became angry with God because we thought God should have taken all our problems away. We did not understand that our Higher Power was there for us all along to offer us guidance, but we needed to be *self-supporting* by doing the footwork to make positive changes in our lives. Tradition Seven helps us identify our distorted thinking. When we begin to apply the tools of recovery, we start to see ourselves in a whole new light. We discover how to become more self-supporting and how to make good choices for ourselves.

Taking care of ourselves financially can be a challenging idea for some of us. If we have not yet learned how to manage our money well, we might need to work toward acquiring that skill. Some of us may have relied on contributions from relatives or friends to rescue us, thinking that we could not make it on our own, or being too afraid to try for fear of failure. Some of us were in debt to others, spent money without regard for how much we had in the bank, or ignored the pile of unpaid bills at home; others spent very little on ourselves. With our Higher Power's help, we examine our financial situation and learn to make more thoughtful and healthier choices for ourselves. We experience a new freedom when we consciously decide to manage our finances in a responsible way. When we know how much we have, we can plan for the future. We consider all of our options and do whatever is necessary to take care of ourselves. We stand on our own two feet, but we know we cannot recover from the effects of sexaholism alone. We listen and share in our groups. We ask our sponsor and other members for their insights. We listen and learn from the experiences of others. We ask our Higher Power to show us how to apply their experience, strength, and hope to ourselves. We begin to recognize when we might need additional help, professional or otherwise. This is not a sign of weakness or personal failure but an important part of self-care. We embrace humility as we seek and accept help when it seems prudent. It may take courage to consult with others when we are used to depending only on ourselves, just as it takes courage to surrender an unhealthy dependence on others. This helps us to find the balance between accepting our responsibilities and recognizing our limits.

Through working Tradition Seven, we learn about healthy boundaries and when to say no. We might have taken on more than our share of responsibilities and wanted to hold on to them. We may have harbored resentments against those who did not step up to serve, whether in our group or in other areas of our lives. We might have felt like victims, unappreciated for all of our hard work. An honest self-appraisal with our Higher Power's help will show us our faulty thinking. Maybe we have not said "No" in a long time because we wanted people to like us or we wanted to avoid conflict. Now, when asked, we can simply and politely say, "No," or "No, thank you," or "I'll think about it." If we are not sure, we pause to consider prayerfully if it is reasonable and appropriate to assume that responsibility. We have learned that "No " does not require any further explanation. When we do our fair share, it provides others the opportunity to make their own contributions and frees us to keep the focus on ourselves.

With the guidance of our Higher Power, we gain a new sense of dignity and self-confidence as we recognize our limits, strengthen our boundaries, and accept our responsibilities. We learn to take good care of ourselves in every way and to place our ultimate security in God's hands.

• • •

TRADITION SEVEN QUESTIONS

Every group ought to be fully self-supporting,
declining outside contributions.

1. How is my S-Anon group financially self-supporting? Do we pay rent for our meeting space? If no particular amount is required, how do we determine how much to contribute? Is this a fair amount?

2. Do we contribute to our local Intergroup, if there is one, and to the WSO? How do we decide the amount? How do we respond to the Special Appeals from the WSO?

3. Do I contribute financially to my group as I am able? Do I contribute personally to the WSO? How do I feel about my financial participation?

4. How does my group define service positions and terms of service? Do I step up to serve? Do I willingly let go of a service position when my term is over? If not, why not? How do I feel about doing service in my group?

5. When I or someone else is doing service, does the group cover the expenses incurred? Do I appreciate those who serve? How do I express it?

6. Have I prayerfully considered service beyond my local group? What service positions appeal to me? As I reflect on my talents and available time, where could I best contribute to the fellowship as a whole?

7. How do I handle my own finances? How do I participate with others in making financial decisions? Is there anything I need to do to be able to become more self-supporting?

8. How am I self-supporting emotionally? Do I still depend upon the sexaholic or others for my self-esteem? Do I take responsibility for my own feelings, or do I blame my negative feelings

on the actions of others? Does my happiness depend on others? On my circumstances? On the recovery/sobriety of the sex addict?

9. How do I accept my responsibilities? Do I depend on others to take care of me? Do I take on too much responsibility and not ask for help? Is there a way I can improve in this area?

10. How is good self-care a part of being self-supporting? Do I practice good self-care? How do I accept the help of my Higher Power? Do I listen to the experience, strength, and hope of my sponsor and other members and then reflect on how I can apply that to my life? How do I decide if I need to get outside help, such as from a therapist or religious leader?

11. How do I allow the sexaholic and others the dignity of taking care of themselves? Do I tend to do for them what they can do for themselves? Do I think I know what is best for others? How is this harmful to both them and me?

TRADITION EIGHT

❧

S-Anon Twelfth Step work should remain forever non-professional, but our service centers may employ special workers.

Because of our personal experience, we are in the unique position of being able to reach out to others who also have been affected by sexaholism in a friend or relative. As the "S-Anon Welcome" states, "We would like you to feel that we understand as perhaps few can. We, too, were lonely and frustrated; but here we have found that there is no situation too difficult to be bettered, and no unhappiness too great to be lessened." [11] We know what has helped us to deal with the effects of sex addiction. We can share how applying S-Anon principles to our personal situation has improved our lives and given us hope. However, we do not give advice because we are not experts and cannot know what is best for another member. We do this Twelfth Step work, as guided by a Higher Power, when we reach out by carrying the message of our own recovery. The experiences we have had and the lessons we have learned through our own successes and failures can benefit others on their recovery journey. We offer them a valuable gift when we share the experience, strength, and hope that we have received through working the S-Anon program one day at a time.

None of us is a "professional S-Anon." Rather, we are a fellowship of equals. No one is expected to have all the answers or a

---

[11] *Working the S-Anon Program,* p. 119.

perfect recovery program. Attending meetings for a longer time than other members does not make us experts or grant us any authority, including giving advice. We trust our Higher Power to guide us in what we say or do when we interact with those who seek our help. Together we make up the S-Anon fellowship, helping each other to recover from the effects upon us of the sex addiction of a friend, family member, or anyone else.

When we serve in this way, we give freely, without obligation, compensation, or expectation of anything in return. We share with others what we have received without taking on the responsibility for how they might respond or react to what we say. Likewise, when we hear the experience of others, we can take what we like and leave the rest. Twelfth Step work is spiritual work that we trust our Higher Power to guide. It is never done for compensation of any kind. The only personal gain involved is that it benefits our own growth in recovery. Giving back what we have been given helps us to grow spiritually and emotionally. Since there is no financial gain or motive involved, we do not compromise our credibility. We can trust that other members are truly reaching out to help us and not trying to take advantage of our situation for their own personal profit.

We listen and share simply as S-Anon members, regardless of our profession, occupation, or training. Even if we are helping professionals, such as therapists, attorneys, or clergy, we remember to put aside those roles when we relate to each other as S-Anon members. We come to S-Anon, attend meetings, and reach out to others because we are in need of recovery ourselves. We do not mention any professional titles and roles at meetings. We show up and share as equals; we do not offer advice, therapy, or counseling. While we are free to consult another member on a professional basis outside of S-Anon, we are careful to keep that relationship separate from our interactions as fellow members. We maintain clear boundaries around these distinct roles. We can ask our Higher Power and our sponsor for guidance in these matters. As in all situations, we carefully guard the anonymity of all of our members.

Together with our Higher Power and other members, we can accomplish things that we could not do alone. At S-Anon meetings we come together to heal from the effects upon us of someone else's sex addiction. In our interactions, we keep the focus on ourselves as S-Anon members and on our primary purpose – helping families and friends of sex addicts.

However, there are some tasks that do require paid employees in order to keep certain aspects of the fellowship running efficiently. Through Seventh Tradition donations from members and groups, S-Anon is able to offer consistent service and pay a fair compensation. There are special workers at our World Service Office (WSO): the Executive Director and staff who provide administrative services for the fellowship. These tasks include answering phone calls and emails from inquirers, filling literature orders, and performing bookkeeping duties. WSO employees frequently receive calls from people seeking help. They connect the callers with S-Anon meetings or members rather than perform Twelfth Step work during their hours of employment.

There are additional tasks that are not Twelfth Step work but that are necessary for our program to function well. Our fellowship may employ special workers such as those who maintain the website, format and design the graphics for our publications, and provide legal and accounting services. These positions require special skills for which we may not have volunteers. They also may require a significant amount of time and effort, which could be more than most volunteers are able to give and still be self-supporting.

Both parts of Tradition Eight can also be applied to our lives outside the fellowship. We remember that we all have equal worth, even if we are in a position of authority over others. We show respect to others and avoid controlling and giving advice. We find that even if family, friends or colleagues do ask for our advice, it often works best to simply share only from our own experience what has worked best for us and what has not worked well.

Just as we rely upon the help of our Higher Power to fulfill our responsibilities to our fellowship through Twelfth Step work, we also ask for guidance to fulfill our responsibilities in our personal lives. We balance the amount of time and energy we need to take care of our own needs, along with what we have available to help others. We practice humility as we recognize that there may be some areas where we do not have the time, expertise, or desire to do the job. We can identify the tasks that we can do for ourselves and those for which we could hire special workers or simply ask for help. We do not expect ourselves to have unlimited resources, abilities, and skills.

We offer our Twelfth Step work freely as fellow members, just as it was freely offered to us. In the process, we gain a deep appreciation for the spiritual nature of these interactions as well as the practical contributions of S-Anon's special workers. In our personal lives, we begin to apply this model of freely offering our help, while also recognizing our limitations and asking for help as needed. Through honoring this Tradition, we grow in self-awareness, humility, balance, and respect for others and ourselves.

•   •   •

A caller was referred to me from the S-Anon World Service Office because I have served as an S-Ateen sponsor for several years. The person was a therapist who had some questions about helping a parent talk to her children who were affected by

sexual addiction. She asked if S-Anon had a curriculum to instruct parents about how to talk to their children. I took a breath and prayed for guidance. I explained that S-Anon is not a professional organization. I told her about my own experience of growing up in a home with active sexaholism, and how I have worked the S-Anon program for several years. It was only after that that I became involved with S-Ateen. I explained that only then did I feel ready to be of service by sharing my experience, strength, and hope with young people. I said that the very best gift I have received in that regard has been my own recovery in S-Anon.

The caller said, "I tried suggesting S-Anon to this mother, but she wasn't interested." Again, I was able to respond to this by sharing my own experience: I had found a wonderful therapist before coming to S-Anon. I was happy with her, and I was not looking for a Twelve Step program. She told me that I needed to start attending S-Anon meetings if I wanted to continue seeing her. Today I am very grateful that I followed her advice. Through the S-Anon program, I have found help and healing, especially from all the shame I was carrying.

I am glad that, without giving advice or trying to control the outcome, I was able to convey the message of hope and help that I have received in S-Anon.

• • •

I wanted so much for our home to be a place of warmth, safety, and mutual support for our family. Instead, after returning to work full-time outside the home, I found myself feeling resentful toward my family members. I felt like I was carrying too many of the household responsibilities. I needed help and support for things to run more smoothly. Then I remembered that I could apply the principle of finding a healthy balance through a division of labor as described in Tradition Eight. I identified specific tasks for which I could use help from other members of the family. One idea that I shared seemed to resonate with my boys: "We all, adults and kids alike, have work to do, and all of us are needed in this family." Sometimes they seemed to get it, and when they didn't, I tried to remember the slogan "Progress, not Perfection." All I know is that our household functioned so much better when we each did our part, so that no one person was trying to do it all. Sharing and communicating about these responsibilities were ways that we learned to express our love, respect, and appreciation for each other.

• • •

In my profession, I sometimes come into contact with people affected by another person's sexual addiction. It is challenging for me to keep my Twelfth Step work in S-Anon and my professional work separate. I recently worked with a person who was struggling with the effects of his partner's sex addiction. I told him about S-Anon and the help and hope that are available, but I did this as a professional and not as an S-Anon member. I had to be careful not to cross over into Twelfth Step work. I knew I had to surrender this to my Higher Power. I also was concerned that if he showed up at a meeting and saw me, my anonymity might be broken. I try to remain in my professional role when I'm at work, praying to stay open to guidance in each situation.

I also have to be mindful of this in dealing with my professional colleagues. Some of them, even those familiar with addiction, don't seem to have much insight into this disease. I'm afraid if it seems like I know too much about sex addiction, they will discover my affiliation. Even though I am concerned about maintaining my anonymity as an S-Anon member, I have tried to consider what I can do to make sure other professionals here know about the program. I have shared some S-Anon pamphlets with my colleagues and told them that I know people who have been helped by S-Anon. I have suggested that my S-Anon group send out mailings to local mental health professionals, college health centers, lawyers, and clergy so that they can refer people when appropriate.

Likewise, in my S-Anon meetings or when talking with newcomers, I am careful to keep my profession out of the discussion. I don't want to sound like I am speaking from any kind of professional point of view. I'm glad to humbly admit to my fellow members that I don't have all the answers. When I give myself freely, I have no strings attached. I don't need to worry about being fairly compensated or fully appreciated. The people I'm helping don't have to wonder about my motives. I think Tradition Eight helps our program "Keep It Simple" by separating paid work from carrying the message.

•   •   •

When I walked into my first S-Anon meeting, I was searching for advice on how to fix my marriage. While I did not find advice, I did find a group of people who offered me compassion and support. They encouraged me to keep the focus on myself. As I sat in those early meetings, I began to identify people who had what I wanted and might be able to help me. Eventually, I began to pick up the phone. One member in particular was a tremendous help to me. Every time I called her, she offered a perspective that calmed me and brought me a measure of peace.

I soon found out that she was a member of a helping profession, but the help that she generously gave me was from the S-Anon point of view. She shared as a fellow S-Anon member, not as a professional. It made such a difference to receive this kind of care and concern. She wasn't helping me because I paid her, but as part of her Twelfth Step work. She understood so much of what I was going through because she, too, had been affected by sexaholism. I trusted her because of that and really benefited from her experience, strength, and hope.

•   •   •

One of my jobs at the S-Anon World Service Office is to answer the phone. For many newcomers, a call to the S-Anon World Service Office is the first time they have the strength or opportunity to verbalize the pain caused by sex addiction in their lives. It's not uncommon for inquirers who are reaching out to the WSO to cry. They may have questions about sex addiction recovery statistics or desperately want to know if I, too, have been affected by the painful addiction, if I am still with my spouse, etc. As a recovering spouse of a sex addict, I feel a lot of empathy for these callers. I get it! I called the WSO once myself, looking for help.

Having experienced the wonders of the S-Anon program, I feel a natural inclination to share the hope I have experienced. However, as a paid special worker at the WSO, it's important that I keep Tradition Eight in mind when answering phone calls and emails from newcomers who are in the midst of the chaos that sex addiction brings. Though I can relate to the newcomer, I must always consider that as a paid special worker, my responsibility is to help all inquirers find a meeting, connect with other S-Anon members who are available for phone support, or purchase literature. If I were to spend too much time on the phone offering a listening ear and sharing my experience, strength, and hope with an inquirer, then I may miss an opportunity to answer another call from someone reaching out for help. Sharing my story may also give a false impression that the WSO is a crisis hotline or that what I say may be interpreted to reflect what the S-Anon fellowship believes as a whole. No one person is the voice of S-Anon.

This was a difficult principle to apply when I first began working at the S-Anon World Service Office. I was in pain and still in the midst of grappling with the effects of sex addiction in my own life. Each call I answered was an opportunity to put Tradition Eight into practice by maintaining compassionate boundaries and redirecting inquirers to call S-Anon members on the phone support list or their local group's contact person or helpline. I will always be grateful for the S-Anon members who are available to respond to the pleas for help!

•   •   •

PRACTICING
THESE
PRINCIPLES

❧

We have found that we can relate to other S-Anon members because of the similar effects that sex addiction has had on all of us, even when the details of our stories are different. We have come to meetings as hurt, angry, or confused people with our own struggles and character defects. At first many of us have a difficult time believing the words of the "S-Anon Welcome." We are convinced that our situations are impossible and that our lives will never get better. Our ability to trust has often been harmed by our experiences with a sexaholic. Yet as we keep coming back, we hear the shares of other members who have had similar experiences, and we see how their lives are improving through working the S-Anon program. They freely offer us something different than a professional could because they not only say that our lives can improve; they show us that it is possible by their own example. They inspire us, model hope for us, and encourage us to keep coming back so we can freely receive the gifts of the S-Anon program in our own lives. The fact that they offer all of this to us freely, without charge or expectations, helps us to be more willing to listen and be open to their message. Gradually, we feel a glimmer of hope. We begin to consider that if this program can work for them, perhaps it might work for us as

> *Volunteering to do service also gave me a chance to learn how to work with others by using the spiritual principles of the Twelve Traditions.*[12]

---

[12] *Reflections of Hope*, p. 167.

well. In addition to attending S-Anon meetings and working the S-Anon program, some of us may also choose to seek or continue to receive professional help. However, doing so does not replace the help and encouragement we receive from other S-Anon members.

We may be tempted to place those members who have been in recovery longer or who have been helpful to us on a pedestal, regarding them as "the experts" and expecting them to have all the answers. We do them and ourselves a disservice if that happens. We are all human and will disappoint each other at times. While we appreciate guidance from our sponsors, we still practice good self-care by using what we think will be valuable and leaving anything that does not seem helpful to us. The perceived perfection of another person is not a safe basis for our own recovery. S-Anon recovery is an ongoing process in which we experience progress, not perfection, one day at a time. Our program teaches us that we are all equals as S-Anon members and that only our Higher Power can guide us to solutions for our individual circumstances.

Eventually, we are able to share our recovery journey and offer hope and help to the newcomer. We do this to keep what we have received in S-Anon as well as to help others. Carrying the message is a gift that we share freely. If we were paid to do Twelfth Step work, it would be problematic, both for the person carrying the message and for the person receiving it. The person carrying the message could lose focus on how a Higher Power, the Twelve Steps, and other tools of recovery guide his or her own progress and continued growth. The person hearing the message could erroneously expect that if payment were involved, the message would be from an expert on S-Anon recovery.

Some of us work in helping professions that require us to focus on the problems of others and to expect financial compensation for our time and expertise, as well as appreciation for and agreement with what we recommend. None of these are part of Twelfth Step work. When we "carry the message" of S-Anon, we do not offer advice, professional or otherwise. We trust our Higher Power to guide us in what we say or do when we interact with others. We do our best to keep the focus on ourselves and let go of any expectations. We often find that what we say is exactly what we need to hear ourselves. We share our own experiences in S-Anon. We are careful to avoid diluting Twelfth Step work with outside influences, such as therapies or specific religious or professional ideologies.

We come to recognize that it takes more than Twelfth Step work for our fellowship to thrive. We gain a deep appreciation for those special workers who do the practical work necessary to make sure that S-Anon is available to those seeking help. We can explore ways to express our gratitude to them for all that they do. As we grow in the understanding that paid workers are essential to our program, we often become more willing to participate, if we are able, in regular Seventh Tradition donations and periodic special appeals. Our participation helps ensure that S-Anon can meet its financial responsibilities, including paying employees a fair wage.

We strive to maintain a balance in our personal lives between taking care of ourselves and giving to others. We learn to recognize and ask for what we need. We may have no problem asking for professional help with fixing the refrigerator or car, but asking for and accepting help regarding our marriage, family, finances, or physical, emotional, or mental health issues may not be as easy. We may find it difficult to let go of the need to look good and be the perfect model of recovery or to admit that we do not have all of the answers. We can ask our Higher Power for humility to surrender our pride and ask for guidance and willingness to take whatever action is needed to move gently forward in our recovery.

Tradition Eight enhances our own recovery as we gain a deeper understanding of not only the importance of Twelfth Step work being freely offered, but also the contributions of S-Anon's paid special workers. We can grow and become who God intended us to be. We are equals among equals, helping others and ourselves as we share the message of hope and healing that S-Anon offers to all of us.

•   •   •

TRADITION EIGHT QUESTIONS

Twelfth-Step work should remain forever non-professional, but our service centers may employ special workers.

1. How do I understand the difference between S-Anon Twelfth Step work and the work done by professionals?

2. Where can I find information about the service structure of S-Anon? Why might this be helpful?

3. Am I aware of the work that paid employees do for the S-Anon fellowship? Do I understand the link between my Seventh Tradition donation and the work of the World Service Office?

4. Do I share only my experience, strength, and hope during meeting times? If I were to share what I do for a living, how might that affect others and me?

5. Do I think other people's opinions are more important than my own? Do I place certain members on a pedestal and expect them to have all the answers?

6. How do I support someone going through a tough time? Do I try to fix people who seem to be going through difficult times?

7. How do the members in my meeting create a safe place for helping professionals to find help for themselves?

8. Do I respect the boundaries of S-Anon members who might be helping professionals and keep my interactions with them as fellow S-Anon members on a Twelve Step basis? If I choose to use their professional services outside of the program, do I maintain clarity about our roles and avoid taking advantage of their skills?

9. How can I carry the message of my own recovery in a healthy way? Am I nervous about taking a phone call from a newcomer because I am afraid I won't say the right thing? How do I overcome this?

10. Do I feel the need to look good in my group and to be a perfect model of recovery? Does this stop me from being humble enough to ask for help?

11. How do I apply Tradition Eight to my personal life? Do I tend to tell others what I think they should do? Do I dominate a conversation? Am I able to see everyone as having equal worth? Are there areas where I would benefit from arranging for extra help, either from my family, friends, or paid special workers? Can I accept help graciously when offered?

12. Are there areas where I would benefit from arranging for extra help, either from my family, friends, or paid special workers? Can I accept help graciously when offered?

TRADITION NINE

❧

*Our groups, as such, ought never be organized;
but we may create service boards or committees
directly responsible to those they serve.*

S-Anon groups concentrate on our primary purpose: to carry the
S-Anon message of recovery from the effects upon us of another
person's sexual addiction. In order to accomplish this, our meetings
keep the time spent on group business to a minimum and avoid
focusing on organizational structure. Instead, we devote our time
to reading the meeting materials and other S-Anon Conference
Approved Literature, studying the Steps and other tools of recovery, and sharing our experience, strength, and hope with each other.

However, as a Twelve Step fellowship, we do have some business that requires regular attention. S-Anon has a structure in place
to do this, but it is based upon service rather than organization. We
might be acquainted with clubs and other associations that have
rules or procedures that determine what should be done and who
should do it. Often there is a hierarchy, with ultimate authority
granted to the top position and lesser authority assigned down the
chain of command. However, we come to find that S-Anon is quite
different; it is a fellowship of equals who give of themselves in the
spirit of service.

The S-Anon/S-Ateen service structure consists of two parts.
The traditional arm is made up of Area Delegates (AD) who represent the local groups at the World Service Conference (WSC), where
they and the Board of Trustees make decisions concerning the entire
S-Anon fellowship. The legal arm of S-Anon consists of members of
the Board of Trustees (BOT): the Regional Trustees, World Service

Office Executive Director, BOT Executive Committee, and Chairs of the BOT Standing Committees. Both arms cooperate when needed, participate in joint phone calls during the year, and interact officially at the annual World Service Conference.

S-Anon has bylaws, maintained and updated by the BOT, that are necessary for S-Anon International Family Groups, Inc., to be a legal non-profit entity. The bylaws define the roles of the Board members and the guidelines for voting on changes to how S-Anon conducts the business of the fellowship as a whole. The BOT Standing Committees have responsibility for a particular area of service within the fellowship. As of this writing, they consist of the Executive, Finance, Literature, International Conventions, World Service Conference, Public Information and Outreach, Archives, S-Ateen, and Policy and Service Communications Committees. The entire S-Anon/S-Ateen service structure is designed to ensure that it is directly responsible to the S-Anon fellowship as a whole.

We need many volunteers for our fellowship to function well and carry the message of S-Anon recovery. When we volunteer to serve, we rely on our Twelve Traditions and Twelve Concepts of Service to guide us. We discover the healthy balance of responsibility and authority as described in the Concepts of Service. As Tradition One reminds us, "Our common welfare should come first; personal progress for the greatest number depends upon unity." Tradition Nine places emphasis on service rather than organization to help safeguard our common welfare. Tradition Two clarifies that for our group purpose, our only authority is a loving God as He may express Himself in our group conscience, and that our leaders serve rather than govern. However, the S-Anon Board of Trustees, whose purpose is to serve the entire fellowship, does exercise leadership and has legal responsibility to conduct the business of S-Anon.

A wise and loving Higher Power guides S-Anon to avoid possible complications of power struggles or derailment from our common purpose—to help families and friends of sexaholics. We use the S-Anon/S-Ateen Service Manual, grounded in S-Anon's Twelve Traditions and Twelve Concepts of Service, as a resource rather than a collection of rules. The Service Manual is available on the sanon.org website and is a helpful source of information and guidance.

In our groups, organizational rules could lead to inflexibility or even exclusion of the voices of some of our members. Instead, we use the group conscience process to guide our decisions. This invites all voices to be heard, including the newcomer's, and enables us to be open to a Higher Power's guidance. We do not control, direct, reprimand, or banish members based on an organizational structure. When we share the leadership responsibility, rotating tasks among members, there is no need for any one of us to be in control. We trust our Higher Power to guide us. This spiritual foundation of S-Anon, rather than our structure, is essentially what holds us together.

We seek to maintain a thoughtful balance between adaptability and stability in our service structure. Complete lack of structure would not be conducive to our serenity or to our ability to carry the message of recovery to others. We can be flexible and open to new ideas while still following the principles of the S-Anon program and respecting our three legacies: the Steps, Traditions, and Concepts. Our individual groups are ultimately responsible for S-Anon as a whole. We each have a voice as well as a responsibility to participate when our groups discuss topics that require a decision on any level. Our participation consists of expressing our own views and welcoming, listening to, and thoughtfully considering the views of others. We avoid disorder and irresponsibility by being respectful of other members and by inviting a Higher Power to guide our decisions and actions, allowing the spiritual aspect of the program to lead us. In a group conscience, we strive for consensus but in some cases may abide by a simple majority decision. We discover that order, common sense, and sharing ideas within our fellowship bring about the best outcomes.

Our common purpose unifies the S-Anon fellowship. We do not concern ourselves with how we could govern and rise to positions of authority over each other. We focus, instead, on how we can serve our fellow members. This strengthens our goal of being a true "fellowship of equals" rather than an organization with a chain of command. Unity with fellow members and commitment to our own recovery are guiding principles that foster the health and longevity of our groups. External pressures and differences in our beliefs, styles, and personalities do not interfere with S-Anon's purpose – to help those who suffer from the effects of someone's sexual addiction. We allow our Higher Power to guide us toward unity.

The Traditions are designed to guide our groups and service arms so that the S-Anon program will continue to be available to all who need it. However, the Traditions are not rules, laws, or mandates. Rather, they are suggestions based upon the wisdom of experience. We have no power to enforce them, but we do have a responsibility to speak up lovingly when the principles of the Traditions are not honored. As fellow members, we can remind each other of their importance, while leaving the outcome of those reminders up to our Higher Power. If an S-Anon group chooses not to follow the Traditions, it can hurt the fellowship as a whole, harm our common welfare, and possibly damage the reputation of S-Anon.

Eventually we learn ways to apply Tradition Nine to our lives outside of S-Anon. While other groups to which we belong might not function like our fellowship, we still can remain mindful of the benefits of unity and working together for the common good. We discover we can let go of controlling or thinking we need to have all the solutions. At home or at work, there will be times when rules are necessary for the health and safety of those involved. When we need to enforce rules, we can look for ways to do so with encouraging words and a positive spirit. We can offer our experience to coworkers or other adults and then let them learn to do the task themselves, rather than micromanaging or doing the task for them. As long as responsibilities are met, how they are done may not be our business.

We find that some structure is valuable in our personal lives. Developing some organizational skills can be a tool of recovery and can lead to a sense of calm, peace, and order. We may set aside time for meditation, prayer, a Tenth Step inventory, and other self-care practices. However, expecting perfect organization can create stress and frustration. Being flexible helps us to be open to our Higher Power's plan. As we grow in our awareness and ability to apply recovery principles, we learn to refocus our energy and expectations. We become freer to participate and cooperate in service.

Our relationships with our families and co-workers can benefit from a structure of consistency and shared responsibility. Both in S-Anon and in all areas of our lives, Tradition Nine reminds us of the strength found in gentleness rather than force, the wisdom found in guidance rather than control, and the gifts found in serving rather than governing.

•   •   •

I was in a lot of pain when I first came to the S-Anon program. I wanted to learn how to fix my spouse, which to my way of thinking would have ended my pain. I hoped to do this quickly and then be able to leave the program. Of course, I eventually

Tradition Nine
STORIES

discovered that this plan was not going to work. I had so much more to learn.

The longer I went to meetings and worked the program, the more I began to understand how many people were involved in making S-Anon recovery possible through their generous service. My sponsor encouraged me to view service as an important component of my recovery.

I started with small gestures of service, but gradually I took my turn in a variety of positions in my group, such as treasurer, secretary, and literature chairperson. I also served on a committee that planned a local one-day recovery event. I truly had my eyes opened regarding the amount of effort involved. Although I had attended these events previously, I had no idea how much work went into planning such an event, from picking the name, designing the flyer, selecting a venue, planning the program, finding speakers, and registering the participants to setting up the rooms and providing refreshments. Without the service of many volunteers, none of this could have been accomplished. There were discussions and disagreements, but all were in the spirit of mutual respect for each other's opinions and perspectives. Things did not get done quickly, but I learned to appreciate the process. We forged ahead with the help of our Higher Power. It felt good to give back what I had received from others. Today I can see even more opportunities to serve.

• • •

After I had some experience working my S-Anon recovery program, I was willing and able to serve beyond the group level as Intergroup chairperson. After my first year, no one volunteered to serve in that position, so I continued to do it. At the end of my second year, again, no one stepped up to serve. Respecting the Traditions, I decided to step down, regardless of whether or not we had a volunteer to take over. A more experienced member pointed out that we could rotate the role for each meeting, and that is what we did for the next year. It felt disorganized to me, but we succeeded in carrying out our responsibilities to the fellowship. Our helpline and website remained available so newcomers could find meetings, and we hosted a meeting marathon and retreat. And we did it all without having the structure of a current chairperson for our Intergroup!

I got to practice applying program slogans such as "Let Go and Let God," "First Things First," and "Let It Begin with Me."

• • •

Tradition Nine has helped me learn to trust others in a group and to trust the process. Rotating positions helps me to realize that each person in a group is valuable and has something to offer. My old tendency would have been to remain in a position in which I felt comfortable, or to encourage others to remain in positions they liked. However, because the group rotates positions every six months, I have had the privilege of watching members grow in their recovery and self-confidence. They seemed to gain so much because they stretched themselves to take positions they initially were unsure they could do. It is so rewarding to hear these same members encourage new members by sharing how much serving has benefited them.

Recently, a counseling professional asked me for a contact number of our S-Anon group for her client. I knew this professional personally, so my impulse was to just give her my number and "take care of it" myself. I then recalled the Traditions and that another person currently had the service position of responding to newcomer calls. She was new at taking calls, but I trusted the process and the Higher Power of the group. She handled the call just fine. As she spoke with the newcomer, some questions came up that she could not answer. She kindly told the caller she would find out the answers and get back to her, which she promptly did. If I had made the call, I would have deprived that member of the opportunity for growth that this experience offered her. The group, in turn, had the opportunity to be strengthened through her service and growth in recovery. We gained a much better understanding of how our service positions worked and how to avoid "double-headed management."

• • •

Whenever my home group reads Tradition Nine, I recognize how far we have come in making positive changes to better align ourselves with this Tradition and other principles of the program. After a few months of regular attendance at a local S-Anon meeting, I decided to make it my home group. However, I was still concerned by the fact that one person clearly seemed to be running the meeting. I was confused about this for two reasons: Tradition Nine states, "Our groups, as such, ought never be organized," and "Obstacles to Recovery" states, "We have no dominating authorities or self-appointed leaders."[13] Even so, this woman single-handedly arranged the room, set out the literature, handled all group service roles, and held a number of area positions.

No matter what the topic, she was quick to tell others how things should be done. Since she was so outspoken and led the meeting at least half the time, it was easy to see why many of us assumed she was in charge. After voicing my concerns to my sponsor, I was surprised to learn it had been like that since the group was formed a few years earlier.

At that point, it dawned on me that our group could benefit from studying Tradition Nine. We learned that by sharing responsibility with all members, we could ensure our group's long-term health and viability. We started to gently make positive changes.

We began by praying to the God of our understanding for wisdom on how to approach the matter sensitively. We wanted to gently express our concerns to this longtime S-Anon member

---

[13] *Working the S-Anon Program,* p. 130.

and avoid giving her the impression that we did not appreciate her faithful service. Then we scheduled our group's first-ever business meeting to ask for input from the members about service and other matters of concern. We decided to take a group conscience quarterly from that point on. We also created and circulated "job descriptions" for the group and area service roles. It was exciting to see five members who had never served before enthusiastically volunteer.

Fortunately, our efforts resulted in many positive changes. Through applying Tradition Nine, harmony and serenity returned to our meeting, helping all of us to continue working our S-Anon program individually and as a group.

•   •   •

Applying Tradition Nine was very helpful when a situation arose in my large family. We became aware that one of our sisters was seriously declining, both mentally and physically. She was no longer able to safely live independently or care for herself. Part of our sister's mental decline was her inability to recognize that she needed help. She did not have a spouse or children to care for her, and the family acknowledged that her care was our responsibility. We worked with the county social services; they eventually confirmed that she needed care and agreed to appoint one of us as her legal guardian.

Choosing a guardian was a daunting and difficult decision for all us siblings. We understood that no one had authority over the others, and therefore no one could make important care decisions without input from all. We also understood that getting such a large number of people to agree on every daily decision needed for our sister's care was not an effective way to care for her. We had many sibling meetings and conference calls, during which we discovered who would be willing and able and who had the best skills and experience to be named her guardian. We decided that one of my sisters and I would serve together as guardians. Based on my program experience, I saw that Tradition Nine was important to this decision – "Our groups, as such, ought never be organized;

but we may create service boards or committees directly responsible to those they serve." I stated I would be willing to serve as co-guardian with the understanding that we would need everyone's trust and support. We would consider their input about ongoing care and revisit our agreement as necessary. We could then reevaluate and consider how to improve our plan.

This structure for the care of our sister was quite successful, though there were a couple siblings who had to be reminded on occasion of our agreement, particularly when it was time to place our sister in hospice care. Once reminded, they stuck to our arrangement. This allowed us to provide the best care possible. Without my application of Tradition Nine and numerous other program Traditions and principles, I would not have been able to perform my guardianship role and, at the same time, retain my sanity and good relationships with my siblings. I continue to be grateful for the gifts that this program and my Higher Power have given me!

• • •

PRACTICING
THESE
PRINCIPLES

☞

We may wonder at first how a group could function well without someone in charge or with only minimal organization. The absence of rules in S-Anon may seem strange, especially if we have come from a home where there was a great deal of rule-keeping or, by contrast, very little order or boundaries. However, we discover that order does exist in S-Anon, and indeed, it is a true fellowship of equals. By attracting volunteers to serve, rotating the necessary

> *...those who take part in S-Anon service work are assuming responsibility—not authority.*[14]

service positions, and seeking the guidance of our Higher Power, we are able to keep our doors open and stay connected to and supportive of S-Anon as a whole.

S-Anon groups are built on shared responsibility for service, not on human authority. We do not require other members to tell us what to do or reprimand us if we do it differently than they would. If a task is not done, it is the group that will be affected, and therefore, the group that will need to find a solution. Tradition Four states, "Each group is autonomous, except in matters affecting another group or S-Anon or SA as a whole." With the guidance of the principles of the program, each group can decide how the meeting will flow and how to handle such things as opening the rooms, welcoming newcomers, and paying the rent. We also can form temporary committees to accomplish certain tasks, such as the planning of retreats or conferences.

---

[14] *Working the S-Anon Program,* p. 35.

The spiritual aspect of the program gives us direction and helps us to serve together. Just as we decided in Step Three to turn our will and our lives over to the care of God as we understood Him, in Tradition Nine we turn our groups over to a Higher Power. We make every effort to listen for guidance and steer away from self-will. If we were to allow prestige and ego to get in the way, we might negatively affect our individual and group progress. We can avoid the extremes of trying to control others or considering ourselves victims, as we might have done in the past.

We have both a right and a responsibility to express our opinions in the decision-making process at all levels of the fellowship, from our home groups and Intergroups to our World Service Conference. We also contribute our time, when we are able, as it is important to volunteer to serve as well as to lend our opinions. Previously, we might have been afraid to speak up, or we might have insisted that things only be done our way. We come to realize the importance of expressing our views clearly and lovingly when we think the Traditions are not being honored, even if we are concerned that it could create conflict. We grow in our ability to express our opinions, serve in a respectful manner, and then let go of the outcomes. This experience gives us an opportunity to practice using our voice in the safety of a group that upholds the Traditions, which prepares us to share more effectively in our families, workplaces, and other groups.

We do not have the right to impose our will on others, even if we started a particular S-Anon group. This is also true if we chair a meeting or serve in a leadership position at the group, regional, or national/international level. We hold our meetings in neutral locations so that no one person assumes full responsibility for the group. Members share the sense of ownership by taking turns with tasks such as setting up the meeting space, chairing meetings, ordering literature, and serving as treasurer. Rotating service positions helps us to remain humble and be open to new insights. We hold regular business meetings so that we can deal with group concerns and problems as they arise. Sometimes the regular business discussion can bring to light other concerns. We can be grateful that we have a peaceful and respectful plan in place to address group issues.

Our personal lives benefit when we apply the principles in Tradition Nine. We invite our Higher Power to guide us as we serve, and are served, in our families and in other relationships. Even in circumstances where there are specific rules, we can examine our attitudes toward them. We can approach the rules as opportunities to serve each other in an orderly way rather than as opportunities to control others or boost our own egos. It is valuable for us to recognize how our defects of character can interfere with being of service. As senior family members or more-experienced colleagues, we might think that we know best how all situations should be handled. We can release this need to be in control, yet voice our opinions if asked. We can learn to serve others while still nurturing our own recovery and serenity. We all benefit when we strive to be open and flexible in all our expectations and interactions.

•　•　•

TRADITION NINE QUESTIONS

Our groups, as such, ought never be organized; but we may create service boards or committees directly responsible to those they serve.

1. What does S-Anon's service structure mean to me? How do I see it as different from an organizational structure? How does it benefit our fellowship? How does it benefit me?

2. What is the difference between serving and governing? When I volunteer for a service position, how can I serve and not govern? How am I responsible to those I serve?

3. What have I gained by doing service work in S-Anon? In what ways can I practice patience, kindness, and humility when fulfilling a service commitment in S-Anon or elsewhere?

4. What role does a Higher Power play in this Tradition? How can I lean on my Higher Power regarding organization and responsibility?

5. Have I familiarized myself with the S-Anon service structure and the S-Anon/S-Ateen Service Manual, both of which can be found on the *sanon.org* website? How could this be helpful to me? To my group?

6. What are the service bodies and committees in S-Anon and how are they responsible? Whom do they serve?

7. In what ways can I support people doing service work beyond the group level? Do I resist volunteering beyond the group level? Why?

8. Does my local group keep the service structure simple? Are there ways we could further simplify things? How can I keep things simple in my life, family, and work?

9. How does my group rotate service positions? What can my group do when there appears to be no one willing to take on a service position?

10. How do I speak up when I believe a Tradition is not being honored? Do I do this in a clear, loving, and gentle way, placing principles above personalities?

11. How can I look at this Tradition from the S-Anon point of view? How can I apply this Tradition to my life outside S-Anon?

TRADITION TEN

❧

The S-Anon Family Groups have no opinion on outside issues; hence our name ought never be drawn into public controversy.

Tradition Ten helps to protect S-Anon from controversy and to ensure that it will continue to be available to anyone who has been affected by the sexual addiction of a family member or friend. For this reason, in our meetings we refrain from expressing opinions, whether positive or negative, about any outside issue such as another Twelve Step fellowship, religion, politics, business, charity, or therapy program. Sharing our viewpoints or taking stands on outside issues not only distracts us from our primary purpose, but it also can cause great harm to our fellowship, jeopardizing our ability to be there for all who might seek its help. In fact, at our meetings the "S-Anon Preamble to the Twelve Steps" reminds us, "S-Anon ... does not wish to engage in any controversy; neither endorses nor opposes any causes."[15]

Many controversial issues exist in our world; political, religious, and societal concerns always abound. As individuals, we are entitled to our own opinions on all of them, but as S-Anon members and as a fellowship, we steer clear of expressing any type of opinion on outside issues during an S-Anon meeting. This is true for topics that are unrelated to our fellowship, but it also holds true for those that appear more closely related. For instance, S-Anon does not have any opinion on other programs that also seek to help

---

[15] *Working the S-Anon Program*, p. 120.

those impacted by someone else's sexual addiction. We neither recommend nor discourage attendance at any of these. However, we do ask that, during our meetings, all members speak only from the S-Anon point of view and not mention any affiliation or membership in other Twelve Step fellowships or recovery programs.

Likewise, the S-Anon fellowship has no opinion on any organizations, fellowships, or treatment programs for those with a sexual addiction. If we were to offer public endorsement or criticism, we would open ourselves up to public controversy. Attempting to influence or interfere with other entities could have serious unanticipated consequences. Any ensuing public controversy would divert us from our primary spiritual aim and might discourage potential members from seeking help from our program. It could also alienate the very people who have a need for S-Anon but who may not share the opinions expressed.

In order to foster a meeting environment conducive to recovery, we avoid discussing issues other than those related to recovering from the effects upon us of another person's sexual behavior. Many of us come to S-Anon feeling shattered and broken, seeking a safe haven. We are in need of comfort, understanding, and a calm, supportive atmosphere. If, instead, we were to find conflicts and quarrels, or a focus on topics other than recovery, we could become discouraged and have no desire to return. If divisive issues do arise about the group or S-Anon, we seek help from our Higher Power and resources such as the *S-Anon/S-Ateen Service Manual*. We hold a group conscience to help reconcile our differences and find an agreeable solution.

Our relationships outside of S-Anon also might benefit from applying this Tradition. In some situations, we can have a healthy discussion in which we state our opinions and listen respectfully to the opinions of others without interrupting or trying to change them. Differing opinions can spark interesting conversations, especially if we have an attitude of curiosity rather than rigidity.

However, we try to do our part to avoid quarrelsome interchanges, particularly if they are not relevant to the relationship or situation at hand. With the help of our Higher Power, we learn to distinguish when it is important to speak up, when to let something go, or when it is best to end the conversation. Talking with our sponsor or another S-Anon member may help us determine the best course. We practice good boundaries when we resist getting drawn into outside controversies. In the process, we do our best to find common ground and focus on what unites us rather than on what divides us.

Our negative reactions to events, issues, and personalities over which we have no control have the potential to interfere with our progress. We have learned that it is best to not allow these obstacles to get in the way of our recovery, whether they come from outside or from within our meetings. Therefore, we do all we can to stay on a healthy, direct course guided by a Higher Power and the principles of Tradition Ten.

• • •

A new meeting of another Twelve Step fellowship with a purpose similar to that of S-Anon began in my neighborhood. I decided that I wanted to see what it might have to offer, so I began attending it as well as my S-Anon meeting. I found both

fellowships helpful. However, I soon found myself mixing the two programs in my mind and not always sharing just from the S-Anon point of view at our meetings.

I was still relatively new to the S-Anon program and didn't fully understand the Traditions or the meeting guidelines. I thought that blending the two programs would benefit everyone. When our S-Anon Intergroup announced that it was looking for volunteers to plan the next retreat, I jumped at the chance. I figured it was a great opportunity to offer a combined perspective, which, in my opinion, would be a gift to all.

As we worked on planning the retreat, I was able to convince many of the other committee members to go along with the idea. In fact, we invited two members of the other fellowship to join us. We made a decision to have speakers and use literature from both fellowships. I thought everything was going along splendidly.

Then one of our committee members returned after being out of town. At our next meeting, when she became aware of our earlier decision, she reminded us of Tradition Ten. She pointed out that the plans for the retreat were being influenced by an outside group and were not based solely on the S-Anon point of view. If we were to include literature and speakers from a different fellowship in our S-Anon retreat, we would essentially be offering a favorable opinion of that outside fellowship.

This stirred up controversy and discomfort. To the S-Anon members, it became apparent that the Intergroup could not sponsor an S-Anon retreat that was not solely from the S-Anon point of view. We offered amends to the two members of the other fellowship and disbanded our committee.

I explored the issue with my sponsor, who helped me understand that, by promoting my opinion on an outside issue such as a different but like-minded fellowship, I contributed to creating harmful controversy. I recognized that I needed to make amends to the committee members from both fellowships. Through this painful experience, I now have a deep appreciation of how important it is that I do not promote my opinions on outside issues, including other recovery fellowships.

•   •   •

Several years ago, I learned an important lesson about Tradition Ten. Before S-Anon began holding an annual World Service Conference, we used to have a business meeting during the weekend of the S-Anon International Convention. At one point there was debate within Sexaholics Anonymous regarding a particular principle. At our business meeting I asked how their decision would affect S-Anon. A more experienced member responded that any business of a different fellowship is an outside issue for S-Anon. He reminded us that Tradition Ten states, "The S-Anon Family Groups have no opinion on outside issues…." He explained that while we may cooperate with another fellowship in planning International Conventions, we do not become involved in their business. If S-Anon had mistakenly offered an opinion on this, it could have harmed our unity within the S-Anon fellowship. It could have also interfered with our working relationships in planning future recovery events.

I am learning how to avoid creating controversy in my group by not expressing my opinions on anything besides our own fellowship. This helps us keep the focus on our own business. I also realize that by staying on my side of the street in my personal and professional relationships, I can avoid a lot of unnecessary trouble. I am grateful to my fellow member for clarifying this Tradition.

•   •   •

During the first year or so that I was in S-Anon, I frequently compared myself to some of the other members. One member in particular seemed articulate and well-informed about the principles of the program and how to apply them to her situation. My self-esteem had been so negatively affected by living with active sexual addiction that I sometimes thought my shares were not as worthwhile as hers. I so wanted to share in a way that would help others as much as she helped me.

In my professional experience, I had been accustomed to supporting my opinions or proposals with information from outside sources. I thought I needed to do this to add to my credibility and to be taken seriously. I carried this attitude right over to my sharing at S-Anon. I would back up my share with advice I had received from my therapist or a book (not Conference Approved Literature) or some other outside source of information that I thought would be helpful.

In the process of studying the Steps and Traditions with my sponsor, I gained a deeper understanding of my motives. I also realized that by expressing my favorable opinions about these outside sources, I actually had been endorsing them. Now, by keeping Tradition Ten in mind, during meetings I share only from the S-Anon point of view and avoid confusion or controversy.

• • •

One of my more painful experiences with the impact of outside issues on S-Anon occurred with my sponsor. After I had been in the program for a number of years, we expanded our relationship into sharing some religious experiences together. This worked fine when our religious beliefs matched, but it did not work well when we no longer shared the same views.

A problem arose when my sponsor suggested that we write a joint version of the Seventh Step prayer. She wanted to base it upon a particular religious belief with which I disagreed. I told her I felt very uncomfortable with her suggestion. All of this disrupted our relationship and my progress in working the Steps with her. I wished that we had never brought an outside issue such as religion into our sponsor/sponsee relationship.

I learned an important lesson that I now apply to myself as a sponsor. Although I may attend weddings, funerals, and other events to support my sponsees, during our one-on-one conversations about recovery, I keep my focus on S-Anon principles. I am grateful for the wise guidance of Tradition Ten.

• • •

My sister is a widow, and both her children are grown and living on their own. For the past seven years, she has dated the same man. My mother has never approved of him. He rarely attends family gatherings, so my mother has had very little contact with him. However, she still frequently gossiped with me about him and my sister. I was uncomfortable with this. I thought about setting boundaries with her, but I wasn't sure exactly what to do.

One day it occurred to me that I could practice Tradition Ten with this issue. Now, whenever my mother wants to talk about my sister and this man, I remind her that their relationship has no direct effect on either of us, so it is an outside issue. It is out of our control, and I don't wish to discuss it. I do not expect my mother to understand Tradition Ten, but I certainly have a clearer understanding of it because of this experience. I am now better able to apply this wisdom to help me set healthy boundaries and avoid engaging in gossip with my mother or anyone else.

• • •

I was a member of S-Anon for quite a while before I recognized that I could apply Tradition Ten to my relationship with my brother. I loved him dearly, but as we grew older, we began to argue over many topics, especially religion and politics. It seemed to me that when we talked, he always tried to promote his opinions and convince me to agree with him. I thought I knew better and that my opinions were superior to his, so I did all that I could to explain the flaws I saw in his reasoning. Eventually it dawned on me that I was doing the very same thing I accused him of doing.

I began to see how damaging this behavior was to our relationship. We would both get frustrated and angry, so our calls did not always end on a positive note. I am slowly learning to be a better listener, not interrupt, and express my views in a calm and measured tone. Because of this, our talks go more smoothly now, even if we disagree. If the topic at hand is a family issue, we discuss it, but we get along better when we don't discuss religion or politics. If he mentions one of these, I can simply change the subject. Instead, we can fondly reminisce about our childhood or share a laugh over the latest escapades of our grandkids. Tradition Ten offered the guidance I needed to respect and enjoy my brother once again.

•   •   •

PRACTICING
THESE
PRINCIPLES

ॐ

Tradition Ten helps us keep the focus on our primary spiritual aim rather than getting distracted by other concerns. By keeping outside issues outside, we avoid controversy and division within our group. Aside from sharing in general terms for a newcomer's sake what brought us to S-Anon, we do not discuss the addict and his or her specific behavior, as that is an outside issue. Those details can vary greatly and can point out the differences in our stories rather than what we have in common—recovery from the effects upon us of someone's sexual addiction. Instead, we focus on what unites us—our common solution. If, however, certain events or situations trigger strong feelings, we can talk about them outside of the meeting with our sponsor or another member.

> *Discussion of outside issues, especially in the context of an S-Anon meeting, can divert us from our primary spiritual aim—helping family members and friends of sexaholics.*[16]

We want our shares during a meeting to reflect the S-Anon point of view. Sometimes our understanding of a particular S-Anon principle is enhanced by something outside the program, such as from a therapist or outside literature. We can share this understanding as long as we do not identify the outside source, either specifically or indirectly in a way that makes the source obvious.

Some of us came to S-Anon so consumed with our own painful situation that we found it difficult to focus on anything else. As we

---

[16] *Working the S-Anon Program,* p. 36.

recover, we stop allowing it to monopolize all our attention. We begin to see beyond our own situation. We may find that we are becoming so enthusiastic or obsessed about an outside issue that we feel compelled to talk about it during our S-Anon meetings. We might mistakenly think that in such a supportive atmosphere it is appropriate to discuss any topic, controversial or not. We can ask our Higher Power for guidance about possible settings outside of the meeting to discuss this subject.

If we decide to express our opinions about recovery or sexual addiction in any setting, whether inside or outside a meeting, it is important that we do not claim to speak for S-Anon as a whole. No one person is the voice of S-Anon.

Perhaps we have some family members or co-workers who have extremely strong opinions on religion or politics that run counter to ours. An intense desire to change someone's opinion on an issue that is important to us could easily turn into an attempt to control. Instead, we can learn to listen to others even when we disagree, and we afford them the same kind of attention we appreciate receiving ourselves. We may use this as an opportunity to consider an alternate viewpoint and to show respect and love. We recognize that we all are entitled to our own views and beliefs, and the fact that they differ does not make either of us wrong. We can take what we like and leave the rest. If we feel ourselves being drawn into an argument, we can choose not to participate. We can use the principles of the program to find a balance. While we may not agree with another person's stance, we can still practice courtesy, even if we decide to leave the discussion.

We might find that applying this Tradition can be more challenging in our interactions with those closest to us. For instance, we may find it difficult to listen to concerns about our behavior from the sexaholic or family members. We might think that they have no right to express a negative opinion, considering their own past behavior. We might feel self-righteous and indignant, become dismissive, and bring up a list of our own grievances. Instead, with the gifts of recovery, we can examine our own attitudes and behaviors. We can ask our Higher Power to help us not overreact and learn to listen and respond respectfully. We recognize that recovery is a process, so we celebrate progress not perfection, one day at a time.

Implementing the spirit of this Tradition can positively affect all our interactions. We pay attention to the person and issue at hand. In some situations, we may need to speak up and clearly state our feelings and opinions. In others, it may be better not to discuss controversial or extraneous topics. We can seek our Higher Power's guidance as to when it is helpful to say something and if it is, how to approach the discussion in a positive way.

We focus on what is truly important in our lives. If we are clear about what is our business and stay out of the business of others, we can avoid turning conflicts into controversy. We find the slogan "Live and Let Live" offers wise guidance in practicing Tradition Ten with our fellow S-Anon members, our loved ones, and everyone else.

•   •   •

TRADITION TEN QUESTIONS

The S-Anon Family Groups have no opinion on outside issues; hence our name ought never be drawn into public controversy.

1. What are some examples of outside issues? What public controversy might these issues create?

2. What is S-Anon's primary spiritual aim? How can discussing opinions on outside issues interfere with our spiritual aim?

3. How can I avoid giving others the impression that there is an official S-Anon opinion about treatment centers, various therapies, self-help books, or other programs?

4. How can I share from the S-Anon point of view about an item from a source outside of S-Anon that has assisted my recovery without directly or indirectly identifying or referring to the source? How can I focus solely on the underlying message or lesson?

5. Have I ever ignored the value of Tradition Ten? If so, what was my motivation? How can I avoid doing this in the future?

6. If outside issues are raised during a meeting, how could I gently bring the discussion back to the S-Anon point of view? How has our group handled this?

7. How do I help foster a calm, supportive environment in our meetings?

8. Where and when is it appropriate to share my opinions on outside issues?

9. How might I use the spiritual principles of Tradition Ten in my personal life as well as in my S-Anon meetings? How can I remember to ask my Higher Power about what to say and how to say it?

10. What choices do I have when I sense that an amiable discussion is turning into a quarrel? What can I do if I feel like I am being drawn into an argument?

TRADITION ELEVEN

❧

Our public relations policy is based on attraction
rather than promotion; we need always
maintain personal anonymity at the level of
press, radio, TV, and films.
We need guard with special care the anonymity
of all S-Anon and SA members.

Once we have experienced the gifts of working the S-Anon program, some of us become eager to spread the good news of recovery with others outside of the fellowship. Our shared experience has revealed that despite our good intentions, attraction rather than promotion works more effectively. The positive changes other people see in us over time speak more eloquently about the benefits of the program than any persuasive words or promises we may offer. Others might notice and ask about the transformation they see in our lives.

Of course, not everyone has the opportunity to see how our individual lives have improved, so we seek to make information about S-Anon available to all who might want help. While some people find S-Anon by talking with an S-Anon member or a friend, others receive a referral from a professional, such as a spiritual advisor or therapist. Still others find our meetings through various sources such as the S-Anon World Service Office website (sanon. org), area websites, telephone helplines, posters, and health fairs. They may also receive information as a result of letter writing and other outreach efforts by S-Anon groups to therapists, healthcare professionals, spiritual leaders, attorneys, human services organizations, advice columnists, advice-related and health-related television and radio broadcasts, other types of media, human resources departments, and correctional institutions.

Offering information about the S-Anon program is not the same as promoting it. Promotion, like advertising, is presenting a message in a manner that conveys it is something others should embrace. Attraction, instead, is making information about S-Anon available to people or organizations and allowing them to decide whether and how to use the information. With the help of our Higher Power, we do our part to carry the S-Anon message in various ways to fulfill our primary purpose—helping families and friends of sexaholics.

In terms of attraction, when those in need of help do make their way to our meetings, what happens next is crucial. A warm smile upon arrival, a reminder at the close of the meeting to "keep coming back," and a friendly conversation with a member afterward can go a long way to foster a sense of belonging. If meetings are held remotely by phone or virtual format, we do all we can to extend the same warm welcome. We try to honor the principles so that S-Anon is a safe haven. We protect the anonymity of all S-Anon and all SA members and do not mention them by name or share details of their stories. We offer good will, comfort, hope, and a gentle invitation to join us on our recovery journey. Newcomers can be encouraged when they see that others coping with similar circumstances seem calm, serene, and may even have a sense of humor.

Outside our meetings, it is essential that we maintain our personal anonymity if we discuss S-Anon in press, film, radio, TV, internet, or any other form of print or electronic public or social media. S-Anon has guidelines to help us in our interactions with such outside entities. These guidelines and other resources can be found on the sanon.org website in the "Members / Public Outreach" section and in the booklet, *S-Anon: A Guide to Public Information & Outreach*. We share as anonymous individuals, not as spokespersons for S-Anon. Revealing our identities could convey a detrimental message that we are experts or authorities. It also would compromise the anonymity of the sex addict and our families, which might put them in jeopardy. It also could be harmful to our own recovery if our egos get involved and we speak from a position of pride rather than humility. Neither praise nor personal gain would benefit us, so we remain anonymous and make it clear that we do not represent S-Anon as a whole when we share information about the S-Anon program.

The principles in Tradition Eleven can also benefit our personal lives. Attraction rather than promotion is a valuable suggestion in all our relationships. When differing points of view arise, we might be tempted to push, prod, or persuade others to agree with us. Instead, we find that a more respectful approach is to simply listen without interrupting, offer our point of view, and let go of the outcome. They may or may not find our ideas attractive. How they react or respond is not our business, but our ability to be humble and serene, even in the midst of a conflict, is very much our business.

Attraction rather than promotion is an effective way to appeal to and engage others. We learn that talking about S-Anon is not a substitute for authentically living the program and practicing its principles in all our affairs. With the help of our Higher Power, we can become more genuine—although never perfect—examples of recovery. We are grateful to find that we can inspire others to begin their own recovery journey. In the Third Step Prayer, we humbly ask the God of our understanding to "Take away my difficulties, that victory over them may bear witness to those I would help of Thy Power, Thy love, and Thy way of life."[17]

• • •

---

[17] *Alcoholics Anonymous*, p. 63.

I am grateful for an opportunity I had to practice this Tradition, along with Step Twelve. An SA member and I presented information about our fellowships to a group of professional counselors and religious leaders. The format was to briefly tell our  stories and then give the attendees time to ask questions about sexual addiction, its effects on family and friends, and recovery. I took great care to only share my story and not any details of my spouse's story. I told them how I had been affected by sexual addiction throughout my life—what it was like, what happened, and what my life is like today.

I was surprised that the professionals seemed to have more questions for me regarding S-Anon than they did for the SA member. They asked about the effects of sexual addiction on me, and why I believed that we in S-Anon also had a disease. I aimed to speak only from the S-Anon point of view. I shared with them how some of the effects that I had experienced left me angry, depressed, and in despair. I told them how reasoning alone did not stop me from repeatedly recalling the shock of discovering this secret addiction. Through working Steps One, Two, and Three over and over again, and then going on to work all the subsequent Steps, I was released from the trauma of rehashing the painful details of another person's acting out behaviors.

Even though initially I felt anxious about speaking, I wanted to be of service to God and others. I knew I was able to share my story safely in this setting because I believed the professionals and others there understood the principle of anonymity and would hold my identity and story in confidence. I was pleased to see by the respect they showed me and by their questions that they were attracted to the S-Anon program through hearing an honest and sincere story of a changed life.

• • •

My spouse and I both had been working our individual recovery programs for several years when our faith community planned a series on various types of addiction. Since our children were grown, we felt free to discuss the possibility of sharing our stories. We recognized that we needed to get each other's permission to break our anonymity in order for both of us to speak in this large public setting.

We decided together to use the event as a chance to shine a light on this stigmatized addiction. We each spoke, in general terms, about our journeys in recovery, mine in S-Anon and my spouse's in his program. We indicated that we would welcome contact from anyone who would like to gain further understanding of sexual addiction and its effects on the family. We offered a message of hope and help that was graciously received. We were grateful for this opportunity to serve.

•   •   •

When I was the coordinator for our local helpline number, one of our volunteers referred a call to me from a TV show. The producers wanted to do a program on infidelity and sex addiction and to include an interview with an S-Anon member. They promised to protect the identity of the participant by changing the voice and not showing the face. They assured us that the identity of the person would not be printed, broadcast, or posted publicly, including on the Internet. They would make the sanon.org website and local helpline phone number available as resources for the audience. Only the producers would have identifying information about the S-Anon member.

I discussed this with my group, and one member volunteered. Later, as many of us watched the program, we noticed that the camera showed the back of our member's head. We were concerned because she had a distinctive hair color and style that could have led to her loss of anonymity. We considered what we could do to protect our members in this type of situation. We reviewed the resources available in the "Public Outreach" section of the S-Anon website for guidance. In the future, we will keep this situation in mind during the preliminary discussions with the media. We cannot foresee all outcomes, but we can learn from our experience.

• • •

Once I have found something to be useful or helpful, I like to share it with my friends and family. This was the case when I first came to S-Anon and began working the Twelve Steps. They were powerful and, among many other things, deepened my faith in my Higher Power. They began to change my whole outlook on life and myself. I was so enthusiastic that I began telling people to work the Twelve Steps, so they could receive the gifts that I had found in the program.

I often was met with some resistance or indifference. I talked with my sponsor, who helped me to see that what I was doing might have come from my strong desire to control others. I also learned that "when the student is ready, the teacher arrives." I stopped promoting the Twelve Steps. I could let my life, hopefully a changed life, be attraction enough. Eventually some friends noticed that I seemed more at ease and asked me about it.

I was faced with a dilemma of how to share the exciting recovery work I was doing without violating my husband's anonymity and revealing his problem with sexual addiction. I had learned years before that neither his story nor anyone else's was mine to tell. A key principle of our program is protecting anonymity—mine and others'.

When my close friends asked me questions, I said I was attending Twelve Step meetings and found them to be very enlightening and supportive of my faith in my Higher Power. I shared some general principles I was learning. I said that the meetings had helped me become aware of my tendency to want to control others. If they asked more specific questions, I told them I preferred not to share those details. In all of this, I was careful not to disclose my spouse's addiction and to keep the focus on myself and my personal growth.

• • •

I wrote a letter to the editor of a large city newspaper regarding an article that involved sexual addiction. I shared briefly that I had found help and support in S-Anon from the negative impact of the sexual behavior of another person. I also provided the address of the S-Anon website. I asked her to not include my last name if she was going to use my letter. She contacted me and said that she would like to use the letter. She clarified that she understood the principle of anonymity within Twelve Step fellowships and would only use my first name and last initial. I have written letters to editors more than once regarding articles about sexual concerns. I find it a good way for me to carry the message of recovery in S-Anon and protect the anonymity of all concerned.

• • •

A ttraction rather than promotion was a difficult idea for me to embrace. A problem came up at work that affected many employees, and I felt very strongly that I had a good solution for all involved. I was brought up to promote my opinion, to try to get others to agree with whatever I thought was the best way to handle a situation. I presented my plan to my boss, who seemed pleased and said she would discuss my proposal with the other managers.

I wanted immediate agreement, so I was not satisfied with this response. I then promoted my ideas to all my coworkers. Some agreed with me and some did not. I pursued those that did not, trying very hard to get them to understand what I saw as the wisdom of my plan. Unfortunately, my approach alienated several people, including some key individuals involved in making the decision. To my dismay, my suggestion was not adopted.

I discussed my anger and disappointment with my boss, who had seemed excited about my plan when I first presented it. She said that if I had just presented the idea and had demonstrated its advantages through my own behavior, the outcome might have been favorable. She shared that my aggressive pursuit had worked against my solution being adopted. Perhaps if I had applied the principle of attraction rather than promotion and let go of the outcome, things would have turned out differently. Even if things had turned out the same way, I would not have jeopardized my serenity over the situation.

• • •

PRACTICING
THESE
PRINCIPLES

෧

If we hear that someone is affected by a problem of sexaholism in a relative or friend, we have a responsibility to carry the message of S-Anon. In certain circumstances, we may choose to break our anonymity. However, to maintain our anonymity, we could mention, for example, that we know someone who has been helped by the S-Anon program, which is certainly true. We can suggest that more information is available on the website.

Making our group welcoming and safe for all members to share is how we practice anonymity to the best of our ability.[18]

We respect the rights of others to make choices for themselves, and we remember that we do not know what is best for someone else. We do not force the program on anyone, but instead offer a sense of freedom and respect when we say at every meeting that the entire program is suggested. We state, "Take what you like, and leave the rest." It would not be healthy for us individually or for S-Anon as a whole if we were to promote a program of recovery to those that we presume need it. We may discover that they do not want it, so we leave the outcome of our outreach efforts to their Higher Power.

We appreciate that attraction brings newcomers to our program, but attraction is also important if they are to keep coming back. We need to be aware of how we greet and treat newcomers at meetings, whether in person or virtual. If we have been coming

---

[18] *Reflections of Hope,* p. 213.

for a while, we might feel a bond with some other members and want to talk with them after the meeting. While this is natural, it is important to reach out and offer newcomers compassion and understanding after the meeting, as well. When we answer their questions, we try to offer clear and simple explanations and avoid the use of any particular recovery terms that might not have any meaning for newcomers. Some groups have special meetings for newcomers or offer them the opportunity to meet with a member one-on-one in a separate room. In other meetings, members offer a brief summary of what brought them to S-Anon, which can help newcomers realize they are not alone.

We listen attentively to those who come to their first meetings. Few of us can be reasoned or argued into recovery, but when we hear open and honest sharing, we often begin to feel hope and a willingness to open up. We learn that we are not alone in this problem and that we can experience love, acceptance, and understanding from our fellow members. An offer of a phone call during the week, even if declined, can convey that we care. We balance our approach and try to be welcoming without coming on too strongly. We do our best to create an atmosphere that encourages newcomers to return.

We try to nurture a sense of trust and safety for all members. Newcomers are invited but not pressured to share, and they are free to open up at their own pace. Fear of having their stories or identities revealed can be a major roadblock for newcomers; the more comfortable and protected they feel, the more willing they might be to overcome their reluctance, share openly, and embrace recovery. We assure them that no observers are allowed at our meetings; only those whose lives have been affected by the sexual addiction of someone else may attend. We emphasize the importance of maintaining confidentiality at every type of meeting, whether face-to-face, phone, or virtual. To protect our privacy, no visual or audio recordings are allowed at meetings. (Conventions and other special events may make audio recordings of certain sessions but will clearly announce this so that anyone wishing to speak or share will be aware of this in advance.)

Tradition Eleven guides us to guard our anonymity as individuals but not to keep the S-Anon program anonymous. We want potential members to be able to find our meetings. This means we do all we can to make information about S-Anon available to those who still suffer. One way we can do this is through the media, and we have guidelines to follow for doing so. For instance, if we are going to be on a television program, we take care to discuss the appropriate anonymity guidelines beforehand with the media personnel; we try to make sure they understand and agree. During any broadcast, we avoid using our full names and presenting images and sounds that might make us recognizable by appearance or voice. Making arrangements with the media involves a certain amount of unpredictability, so if we are to proceed, we need to be aware of the possibility of human error.

In public forums of any kind, we must ensure that we protect our anonymity for two reasons: to not reveal our personal identity and to not appear as a representative of S-Anon. We clarify that we are speaking about our individual experience in S-Anon, but we avoid appearing to be a spokesperson for the S-Anon program. Because we are a fellowship of equals, no one person can speak for us all.

We take special care to guard the anonymity of those who are in recovery for sexual addiction as well as S-Anon members. An unintentional careless word can cause harm. Deliberate discussions or gossip about other people, whether inside or outside our meetings, are detrimental to all involved. Because of the effects of living with this disease, especially having low self-esteem and feeling isolated, we can be tempted to participate in gossip in order not to feel left out. One appeal of gossip is that it might give us a stronger sense of belonging. However, we find that it diverts us from our primary spiritual aim by taking our focus off ourselves and leads to the need for us to make amends. If we want to help create a safe atmosphere, we avoid talking about other people. We accept that they will make mistakes, just as we do. We also protect anything that someone shares in confidence with us. With the help of our Higher Power, we learn to practice a higher degree of respect for others and ourselves.

We might have a natural tendency to protect our own anonymity and that of fellow S-Anon members, but we may not necessarily be as concerned about protecting the sex addict's identity. We

Tradition Eleven

might, in an effort to find understanding and ease our pain, end up revealing information without thinking about the harm it could cause. Maybe we impulsively want to vent our frustration without considering if our audience is appropriate. On the other hand, perhaps we want to seek revenge, to punish and shame the sex addict by deliberately disclosing his or her behavior to others. These actions are not in our best interest, nor in the best interest of the sexaholic, and frequently have larger, unintended consequences. Maintaining anonymity is particularly important with sexual addiction due to the stigma that impacts all involved. Because we might experience these or other detrimental inclinations, the guidance of Tradition Eleven—to take extra care and to be especially mindful of anonymity—is valuable in keeping ourselves and our actions in line with our program of recovery.

Both attraction and anonymity are important principles to practice outside of the fellowship as well. Our tendency to want to control how others respond can be tempered by the principle of attraction. Perhaps we want others to do things our way and try to promote our ideas of how things should be done. Eventually we find that the principle of attraction and an example of a life well-lived can be much more powerful ways to carry the message of recovery.

• • •

TRADITION ELEVEN QUESTIONS

Our public relations policy is based on attraction rather than promotion; we need always maintain personal anonymity at the level of press, radio, TV, and films. We need guard with special care the anonymity of all S-Anon and SA members.

1. What is the difference between "attraction" and "promotion?" How does the way I work my program attract others?

2. If others outside the program ask about my serenity, how do I decide whether or not to share about S-Anon? If I decide to share my recovery, how do I do this?

3. Have I ever knowingly promoted S-Anon? Have I tried to pressure family members or friends to enter recovery? By doing so, how might this have made S-Anon unattractive to anyone listening?

4. How does my group create a welcoming atmosphere? Are there ways we could improve?

5. In regard to attraction, do the newcomers in my meeting hear me honestly share my experience, strength, and hope when I speak? How do I share that the program "works when you work it?"

6. How is my group helping to inform the general public and the health community about S-Anon? How are we careful to protect our anonymity as we do this? Am I familiar with the resources that S-Anon offers, such as the information on the sanon.org website, the pamphlet *Information for Professionals*, and the booklet *S-Anon: A Guide to Public Information and Outreach*?

7. What does "special care" mean in the context of Tradition Eleven? How do I protect the anonymity of the people in my meetings? How do we keep our meetings safe?

8. Why should I be concerned about the anonymity of S-Anon and SA members? Do I extend this concern to those who might be in a different program or who are not in recovery? Why is anonymity important to me personally?

9. What could happen to S-Anon if we did not practice Tradition Eleven? How does my membership and the health of my group affect the worldwide fellowship of S-Anon?

10. How is Tradition Eleven helpful in my home, work, and social life? How does adhering to it help me in all my relationships?

TRADITION TWELVE

॰ॐ॰

*Anonymity is the spiritual foundation of
all our Traditions, ever reminding us to place
principles above personalities.*

As we study Tradition Twelve, we come to understand how the
spiritual principle of anonymity is of fundamental importance
to each one of our Traditions. There are several aspects to this
principle, which range from considering our common welfare to
respecting the anonymity of others to participating anonymously
as an equal among equals. We guard the anonymity of our fellow
S-Anon members, the sexaholic, and ourselves. We maintain our
own anonymity in meetings by not revealing our last names, but
also in a larger sense, by not divulging other parts of our lives that
could distract us from our purpose or divide us rather than unite
us. We are all simply individuals seeking a solution to our common
problem of being affected by the sex addiction of another person.
Our outside identities have no relevance to our membership in
S-Anon. With our Higher Power's help, we can show respect for
other members, humbly participate as a member among members,
and honor all aspects of anonymity.

We hold everything that is said and everyone who is present
at a meeting in confidence. A reminder card at our meetings helps
us stay attentive to this principle: "Whom You See Here—What Is
Said Here—When You Leave Here—Let It Stay Here." When we
keep these words in mind, we protect the anonymity of everyone.
We are careful not to repeat what we hear, even from a good friend
in the program to a mutual program friend, unless we have permission. What we hear at a meeting or in a private conversation with

an S-Anon friend is there to help us. We keep it in our hearts and minds to guide us on our recovery journey.

We also have guidelines for sharing during our meetings. We are mindful that the intimate aspects or graphic details of our stories can trigger other members and distract us from focusing on the solution. In the spirit of humility, we take these things to a sponsor or other support person instead of sharing them during a meeting. Likewise, we do not tell another person's story; we share only about our own journey, and we are careful about what we choose to disclose. We can jeopardize anonymity even by mentioning a family member's or a friend's first name. We do not identify anyone by name or specific line of work.

We find that humility is vital to the spiritual principle of anonymity. Humility makes it possible for us to know and accept ourselves and to connect with God and others. With the help of our Higher Power, we strive to surrender our pride, self-centeredness, ego, and desire for prestige and personal recognition. We participate in the S-Anon fellowship as equals, neither superior nor inferior to anyone else. As our recovery progresses, we see how our most basic sense of self-worth comes from our relationship with our Higher Power rather than from the praise or attention of others. Honoring anonymity with humble hearts safeguards all of us.

When we are anonymous, we are free to be our authentic selves. Therefore, we do not have to try to project a certain image of ourselves or maintain a certain status. Anonymity removes labels and expectations that we have placed on ourselves or others. It allows for more honest and transparent exchanges. We do not bring up or discuss outside issues such as education, occupations, politics, religion, or treatment programs; we avoid the use of any vocabulary specific to these areas. When we meet as fellow members dealing with our common problem, we discover that help and hope are available to all people affected by sex addiction. We make our S-Anon recovery journey together, not in isolation, yet we are free to travel in our own time and our own way.

As we do service in S-Anon for the group or beyond, we do so as trusted servants and ask our Higher Power to help us let go of any attempt to control. Our goal is not to prove ourselves right or get the group to agree with us. We gain confidence that our opinions are worthy of being heard and considered by the group, but we voice our opinions without insisting on our own way. We learn not to take things too personally by realizing that "principles above personalities" even includes our own personality. We then trust God to reveal the outcome as expressed in the group conscience. In the process, we learn to live humbly, at peace with ourselves and with others.

Since we all have unique personalities and preferences, differences of opinion are bound to occur at times. How we handle conflict or disagreement can impact the quality of our relationships. Honoring the common good becomes more important to us than insisting we are right. We do not have to like each other to respect each other; we place principles above personalities. The situations that brought us to S-Anon may be different, but we remember that we are here for a common purpose. We will likely be called upon to consider ideas that are new to us. We listen to the message with an open mind rather than focus on the messenger. We try to listen attentively without filtering it through any preconceived biases. We trust a Higher Power to help us discern wisely.

We are all equal as S-Anon members. The words we need to hear at a particular time do not always come from the member who is leading the meeting or from a long-time member. Mentioning our length of time in S-Anon during our sharing could invite harmful comparisons. We do, however, celebrate members' length of time in S-Anon recovery by acknowledging "birthdays" at some meetings and recovery events. All are equally important and equally celebrated.

The principle of anonymity guides us to serve the fellowship with humility. While we might want to be admired by the group, we have learned that it is detrimental to our own recovery. Believing we deserve recognition stems from pride and can make us vulnerable to envy, criticism, and loneliness. It is equally dangerous to set any individuals on a pedestal or consider them or their recovery superior.

We are grateful for the members who serve us in many ways, such as serving as Area Delegates, organizing S-Anon events, or creating new literature. However, in order to maintain anonymity and our emphasis on "principles above personalities," we focus on the service provided, not on who provided the service. We have a guideline in *Working the S-Anon Program*: "At fellowship gatherings and conventions we practice this principle by listing topics, rather than individual speakers, on flyers and programs. S-Anon is a fellowship of equals—there are no VIPs or 'stars.'"[19]

Likewise, as stated in *Working the S-Anon Program*: "Individuals are not given special recognition as authors of particular pieces of literature, and members are not mentioned by name when personal stories are published."[20] In a larger sense, all of us in S-Anon indirectly influence our literature by sharing our experience, strength, and hope with each other. No one individual could possibly take credit. Anonymity helps us see ourselves as members among members, each of us contributing for the good of the whole in the best way we can.

We can also apply this Tradition to our everyday lives with families, friends, and co-workers. We keep things that are shared with us confidential. Even if we are in positions of authority, we humbly recognize that all people have equal worth. No matter our established role, when we show kindness and respect to all involved, we help any group of people function better. We listen to each other and look for ways we can work together rather than seek higher recognition and status for ourselves. We can be open to each other, apply "principles above personalities" in all situations, and evaluate ideas based on their intrinsic worth rather than on who suggested them. We ask our Higher Power for guidance, seeking unity and peace rather than prestige and prominence.

We practice Tradition Twelve by carefully respecting all aspects of anonymity and remembering to place principles above personalities. We strive to humbly live by our spiritual principles, with the help of our Higher Power, one day at a time. We focus on the message rather than the messenger and relate to others with acceptance and a sense of being connected through a Higher Power.

•   •   •

---

[19] *Working the S-Anon Program*, p. 43.
[20] Ibid.

Iused to be easily distracted, but after going to many S-Anon meetings, I have become a much better listener. I appreciate the wise guidelines we have for sharing during meetings. However, when members do not follow these guidelines and mention their specific travel destinations, pro-

Tradition Twelve
STORIES

fessions, expensive purchases they have made, degrees they have earned, titles they have acquired, and specific pastimes, I find myself making comparisons and judgments rather than listening for their experience, strength, and hope. I can lose my focus and start stereotyping and classifying people.

I also am concerned for any newcomer who may not have certain social advantages and may feel less than. Anonymity is more than just about keeping our last names off our member list. By keeping specific details from my sharing at meetings, I can support our unity as well.

• • •

My spouse went into a treatment center for sex addiction, and at family week, I met someone who was a celebrity. I found myself wanting to tell everyone I knew about meeting him, despite anonymity being addressed during family week. Fortunately, when I returned home and attended S-Anon meetings, anonymity was stressed at every meeting. This led me to decide not to tell anyone about meeting this person.

As I worked the S-Anon program and began examining my own behavior and motives, my desire to tell people about this celebrity encounter came up again. If I am honest with myself, I recognize the reason I would like people to know I met a famous person is because I want them to be impressed and think better of me. When I did my Fourth Step inventory, I figured out why I really want people to like me. I grew up in a home where any imperfection was criticized harshly. I came to believe that I had to appear perfect to be loved and accepted. I was often compared to others. I learned that if I appeared "better than" the people around me, their view of me would be more positive, and I would feel better about myself.

In S-Anon, I have discovered that it feels so good to be in a fellowship of equals. I love feeling accepted just as I am, faults and all. When I tell the group about my mistakes, I feel even more acceptance and love! In my relationships outside of the program, I may not always feel unconditionally loved or accepted, but I try to be who I truly am and respectfully let others be who they truly are. To me, this is practicing humility. When I compare myself to others or pass judgment, I don't feel serene or connected. I feel like I'm right back in my disease. If I find myself thinking I am better than or less than someone else, I start to sense a warning in my gut, telling me I need to work my Steps with my Higher Power around that issue.

I have never revealed the identity of the celebrity I met. Now I practice this principle outside of the meetings, too. I keep what I learn in my interactions with other people confidential. I'm so grateful for Tradition Twelve. At first, I thought anonymity was there only to help me feel safe enough to share my secrets in the meeting. I have learned it is so much more! Anonymity teaches me my true place in relation to others—right there beside them.

• • •

For many years I appreciated anonymity as something that protected me from being identified as an S-Anon member. I could go to meetings, and if I met a member elsewhere, I could trust that my membership in S-Anon would not be revealed.

More recently I have discovered another aspect of anonymity that has helped me grow in a significant way. At times I have enjoyed being in the limelight, desiring people to notice me and my accomplishments. However, I saw that in S-Anon no one person is more important than another. We are all equals. Members who have many years in the program and those who have done a lot of service work don't receive any more recognition than anyone else. My Higher Power has helped me to understand the connection between humility and anonymity.

• • •

I find that studying the Traditions helps clarify many things for me, one of which is who qualifies for the S-Anon program. The first time I heard some members use the term my qualifier and realized they were talking about another person, I was confused. However, I started to use the term myself, even though it didn't feel comfortable. I eventually had to examine why I felt this way. I decided to look up *qualifier* in a dictionary, and it said, "One that satisfies requirements or meets certain standards." The only requirement for membership in S-Anon is being affected by a problem of sexaholism in a relative or friend. I meet this requirement for membership. After study, reflection, and talking it over with my sponsor, I decided I would no longer use the term my *qualifier*. I feel more comfortable now, having decided this for myself. I qualify.

•   •   •

In the past, when I interacted with the overpowering personality of my cousin, I did what I saw modeled for me in my sexaholic family of origin. Either I did whatever she wanted, or I withdrew and wallowed in negativity about her, my family, and myself. Recently, I wanted to give a gift to her son to recognize a special occasion. My cousin, as was her habit, put many obstacles in my path. For whatever reason, she wanted to limit the number of presents he received. To me she seemed to be, yet again, controlling the situation, and I almost gave up. The principle of family connection helped me to persevere; I did not want to lose contact with my cousin or her son.

Instead of giving up or just doing whatever my cousin wanted, I called my sponsor and talked through different options of how to proceed because I wanted to find a way to honor this young man. Family connections are important to me, so I considered how I could apply the principles of the S-Anon program by looking beyond my cousin's personality. I didn't want to continue feeling resentment or anger. I prayed about it and asked God for both guidance and the willingness to follow that guidance. Thankfully, I was then able to discuss the subject of the gift with my cousin respectfully. Instead of assuming I knew what she thought, I told her my wishes, asked for hers, and then carefully listened. I felt a great sense of freedom in doing the right thing because I wanted to, not necessarily because it was easy or because I liked my cousin's personality.

I accepted God's guidance to place principles above personalities, so I was able to give the present in a way that honored my needs and wants as well as my cousin's concerns. I felt good about this and was pleasantly surprised by the gift of an improved relationship between my cousin and me.

•   •   •

PRACTICING
THESE
PRINCIPLES

Humility becomes an integral part of recovery in Step One, and it continues to guide us throughout all the Steps and Traditions. It is a vital component of anonymity and helps us to see ourselves and others more realistically. Humility helps us to be open to solutions that may come to us through working the S-Anon program. When we accept that we do not have all the answers, we become willing to consider a different approach to life and to recognize and seek help from a Power greater than ourselves. Humility makes it easier to embrace all aspects of recovery, such as taking a regular inventory and making amends.

By maintaining anonymity, we are practicing humility in our recovery.[21]

Humility does not mean that our feelings of anger and hurt are not valid, but it helps us recognize that obsessing about them is not beneficial. When some of us came to the fellowship, we may have been filled with thoughts like, "How dare he! How dare she!" We may have been consumed with feeling superior and obsessed with what we thought they deserved. Judging people, including the sex addict and ourselves, blocks our progress. When we can accept that we do not know other people's thoughts or motivations, we find it eases our interactions. Humility helps us recognize our powerlessness over someone's disease and opens up the possibility of receiving the help available in S-Anon and from a Power greater than ourselves. Accepting life on life's terms might be a new concept, and it is one that requires humility to embrace. Learning

---

[21] *Working the S-Anon Program,* p. 37.

to be grateful for what we have instead of focusing on what we don't have requires humility as well. We eventually discover that humility and its partner, gratitude, help us to receive the gifts of the program, including recovering the feeling of joy.

As we progress along our recovery journey, we come to understand that our professions, educational backgrounds, financial status, membership in other recovery programs, etc. do not matter when it comes to recovery with others in S-Anon. This does not mean that we cannot be justifiably proud of our hard work and accomplishments in our personal lives, but rather that these have no bearing on our membership in S-Anon. Likewise, those of us who wish we might have experienced more material, educational, or any other kind of success recognize that this also has no bearing on our membership. In our meetings, we humbly practice anonymity and do not mention these aspects of our lives. In S-Anon we learn to let go of *what* we are and focus on *who* we are.

We come together anonymously to seek a spiritual solution. As we practice anonymity, we develop a deeper understanding of living in relationship with our Higher Power and in harmony with others. What matters is our shared experience as individuals affected by the sex addiction of someone else, which binds us together. We do not place others above us or below us. We all have an equal place in the rooms of S-Anon, and many of us discover a sense of belonging deeper than we may have experienced anywhere else. We avoid mentioning our other identities during our meetings, including membership in any sex addiction or other type of recovery program.

We grow in our ability to act with integrity. For instance, some of us may have had difficulty keeping a confidence in the past, but we discover that it is indeed possible for us to honor anonymity by not participating in gossip and by setting boundaries, respecting the privacy of all, keeping personal stories to ourselves, and surrendering self-centered desires. We develop a sincere respect and appreciation for others and ourselves.

Participating in service also gives us opportunities to practice the principle of anonymity. Before coming to S-Anon, we might have expected compliments from others on our accomplishments. While it is natural to enjoy appreciation, as our sense of self-worth grows in recovery, we can let go of needing external recognition and reward. We do service out of gratitude and out of our desire to support the fellowship and grow in our own recovery. We do this one day at a time, with the help and guidance of our Higher Power. Even when we are hesitant to serve, saying yes when we are able will help us grow in self-confidence. We may learn to do things we otherwise might not have. Our reward comes from the satisfaction of giving back to the program, not from any personal acclaim.

As our understanding of anonymity grows, we realize the importance of placing principles above personalities. We need each other to recover, but we might run into challenges. For instance, we may not agree with everyone who participates at a group conscience meeting. With the help of our Higher Power and the gift of humility, we learn to accept that our opinion may be in the minority and that we will not always get our own way. We listen to the ideas of others, express our own ideas, and then trust the process. Applying "principles above personalities" can help us to let go of the outcome, even if we are initially disappointed.

We may not like everyone, but we try to listen to each other and look for the good in everyone. A person whom we find irritating might offer a perspective that is helpful to us. If we start tuning this person out, we may miss receiving this gift to our recovery. We say, "Take what you like and leave the rest," but we do *not* say, "Take only *from* those you like." Our Higher Power can speak through all of us.

When we remember to place principles above personalities, we can benefit from all our interactions. In most areas of our lives, we are going to run into some personalities that we find challenging. Conflict can occur, but we can help resolve it by employing spiritual principles and looking at what we have in common. We can focus on the issue at hand rather than on the personalities on each side of the issue. We might have the most difficulty with those who have some of the same character defects we have. As the slogan says, "When you spot it, you got it." Recognizing this presents an opportunity for growth if we remember that we are not perfect. Sometimes we gain a keener understanding of the problems our defects can cause when we are on the receiving end. For example, we might better understand the consequences of making critical remarks if we hear them directed at ourselves. We think about how we like to be treated even when our disease is active, and we try to extend the same treatment to others. We can apply the spiritual principle of treating everyone with dignity and respect.

Anonymity reinforces how important it is to focus on what we have in common with any group of people. We can apply anonymity in our lives outside of S-Anon by considering, with our Higher Power's help, how to best recognize and come together around whatever unites us. We can explore how to treat each other with respect, equality, and humility and how to be family members among family members, friends among friends, etc. We can ask God to guide us how to live by these spiritual principles in all areas of our lives.

• • •

TRADITION TWELVE QUESTIONS

Anonymity is the spiritual foundation of all our Traditions, ever reminding us to place principles above personalities.

1. How do I see anonymity as being the spiritual foundation of S-Anon Traditions? What does the *spirit* of anonymity mean to me? Do I remember not to identify anyone or tell an identifiable story, even when I'm speaking to a group member? Do I apply this principle even when a well-known person attends a meeting?

2. Have I ever knowingly or unknowingly broken another person's anonymity? If so, what did I learn from this experience? How do I protect someone's anonymity if I meet her or him outside a meeting? Do I recognize that it is not respecting anonymity to use any term, including "double winner," that identifies an S-Anon member as also being a member of a sex addiction recovery program?

3. How does anonymity support the idea that S-Anon is a fellowship of equals? What does humility have to do with anonymity? Why is it important to surrender any desire for prestige and admiration?

4. How do I pay attention to what I share at meetings so that I observe anonymity? Why is it important that we do not share our occupation, religion, education, membership in any other recovery or therapy programs, etc.? In what ways can I practice the principle of anonymity regarding these outside issues?

5. How can anonymity help me become more mindful of common welfare and unity when relating to others? Do I allow the people in my life to tell their own stories?

6. How am I able to recognize the difference between principles and personalities? How could I discuss a principle without reacting defensively?

7. Am I able to pay attention to *what* is said rather than *who* said it? If I don't like someone, how can I still show respect for that person?

8. How can focusing on principles help me to resolve conflicts? When there is disagreement, how do I practice Tradition Twelve, both during the discussion and afterwards?

9. How important is my anonymity when acting as a trusted servant? Am I willing to focus on principles and not personalities in my service work? Do I take another group member's questions or comments about my service personally? How can I focus on principles and the good of the group or fellowship as a whole?

10. How can I practice anonymity and principles above personalities in my life outside of S-Anon?